# DESERT WARRIOR

REPORTING FROM THE GULF

*a personal account*

Richard Kay is a senior writer with the Daily
Mail. Since 1980 he has successively been Irish
correspondent based for three years in Belfast,
royal correspondent, travelling extensively with
members of the Royal Family, and foreign correspondent with assignments from Afghanistan
to Yugoslavia. He is 36 and lives in London.

*To David,*

# DESERT WARRIOR

REPORTING FROM THE GULF

*a personal account*

*With warm regards,*

*Richard*

*December 25, 1992*

## RICHARD KAY

penumbra books
london

First published in Great Britain 1992
by Penumbra Books
21 Pandora Road London NW6 1TS

Text copyright © Richard Kay
Photography © Mike Moore
All rights reserved

A CIP catalogue record for this title
is available from the British Library

ISBN  0 9520599 0 8

Printed in England by
Commercial Colour Press

# Contents

# Acknowledgements

This book would not have been possible without the journalistic twist of fate which sent me and kept me in Saudi Arabia, my editor Sir David English, for the assignment, and foreign editor Peter Birkett for his unflagging enthusiasm for the enterprise. In Saudi Arabia, Steve Back for his food parcels, David Williams for his Test Match reports and Geoffrey Levy for his encouragement are also in my debt. In London Tim Hine who agreed to publish this book, Sally Hine and my mother for correcting the manuscript and to others who put up with so much: thank you.

My thanks go also to Colonel Iain Johnstone and his men of 1st Royal Scots, notably Major John Potter, Major James Hewitt of the Lifeguards, and Brigadiers Christopher Hammerbeck and Patrick Cordingley, who commanded the 4th and 7th Armoured Brigades.

But my special thanks must go to Mike Moore, an outstanding photographer with Today who was with me throughout and is a true friend.

*And war was declared*

It was four o'clock in the morning
The air was still and cold
The troops were in their baggies
But they had not yet been told.
It started about an hour ago
The boys felt they'd been sold
Those high-ups think that they are so brave and bold.
The thought doesn't amuse me to think what might have been
If one Iraqi bastard had got past the radar screen
Well one thing is for certain
What's here now might not have been.
Can you imagine the confusion
Trying to fight the unseen
We fight for Queen and country
Because that's the job that we pursued
It's the thing that we excel at
We're the best at what we do.
If we continue how we started
Then one thing is for sure
It isn't crystal balls we'll need
It's ESPs for sure.

Poem by Private Ian Courtney
1st Royal Scots

# ASCOT TO DHAHRAN

'YOU'VE ONLY GOT nine seconds to put on your respirator because in ten seconds you are dead.' The black size 2 mask belonged to my Nuclear, Biological and Chemical protection suit and, judging by the RAF man's pained look, I was technically dead half a minute ago. But, I thought, struggling with the awkward rubber straps of the respirator, this is all a bit of a game. After all, I am the Daily Mail's royal correspondent, a job blessed with the better things in life, comfortable executive travel, five-star hotels and always in exotic locations. Windsor Tours, we called it, and this was just another royal visit. Prince Charles was off to give a tonic to the troops in the Gulf and we both would be home for Christmas. Surely, I won't actually have to struggle into one of these green NBC suits even if I am flying to Dhahran, Saudi Arabia, just down the road from the Kuwaiti border and Saddam Hussein's occupying army of Scud missiles primed, we are told, with chemical warheads.

Outside the departure lounge at RAF Brize Norton, a shaft of winter sunshine bathed the yellow stone houses of the village from which the base takes its name with a golden light. Somehow all this brisk barrack-room talk of nerve gases and blister agents seemed faintly absurd. I shot a sidelong look at my fellow-traveller, Ramsay Smith of the Daily Mirror, who had mastered the technique of donning his mask and in his Fleet Street issue navy blazer and slacks, looked like something out of Dr. Who. But the briefing was far from over. The Warrant Officer held up slips of paper, stained with what looked like blackcurrant juice, only the stains were caused by the deadliest chemicals in the world. The one on the left tells you it's a blistering agent. The one on the right, a nerve

1

gas. "This is your early warning system. You put them on your suit like this," he said, slapping the sticky paper on receiving pads over his tunic.

You begin to hope they wouldn't discolour — and presumably in the heat of an air raid that you actually notice — before the next warning system flicks on, muscle twitching, vomiting and blindness. By then it's time for the Compopen, the canisters full of Atrophine tipped with one and a half inch long needles you must drive into your thigh at the first sign of muzziness. For an hour we are given an almost gratuitous catalogue of the horrors of chemical warfare and handed the deterrents that seem flimsily inadequate. Flasks of fuller's earth, packets of pills to build the body's resistance to gases and a spare foil-wrapped canister for the respirator. The kit piled before us assumed mountainous proportions: Two NBC suits of charcoal-lined smock and trousers, two pairs of outer rubber gloves and two inner of cotton, two pairs of clumsy rubber overboots and a haversack containing respirator and attachments. It was, we were assured, the best in the world. But it weighed a ton and the thought of shouldering it like sherpas across the desert drove us in search of a drink.

Gateway House would not rate a mention in any Michelin guide but the RAF establishment was going to be our last chance of purchasing alcohol before our return. In the officers' mess I settled down over a comforting whisky to review why I had the 'good fortune' to be bound for Saudi Arabia in the first place.

Only twenty-four hours earlier I had been covering the Children of Courage awards in Westminster Abbey, an annual jamboree to mark extraordinary deeds by ordinary children. One of them appropriately this time, had been Stuart Lockwood, the bewildered little boy who Saddam used in a television charade a few months earlier. But for the past three years mine had been an altogether gentler journalistic world, chronicling the doings of royalty and society figures. The Derby, Royal Ascot, Henley Regatta and Guards' Polo Club was my beat, liberally dosed with frequent trips abroad pursuing the younger members of the Queen's family .

In a couple of days there would be the christening of the Duke and Duchess of York's new baby to attend, and I was looking forward with relish to those winter skiing trips that royal correspondents see as a reward for all those dull pavement days hunting the chance remark that might propel that day's Royal onto the front pages. So when I walked into the Mail's offices in Kensington that afternoon to be met by an enthusiastic Peter Birkett, the paper's foreign editor, with the news that my name was down to go with Charles to the Gulf my first reaction was one of rather less than unbridled enthusiasm. Diana, I reasoned, was a lot better prospect, off to Germany to see the soldier's wives, good female angles there in a paper that appealed to women — and only a fraction of the cost.

Anyway, all was not lost. The Ministry of Defence announced they intended to operate a pool to cover Charles. One reporter from the Press Association, the national news agency and two to be drawn from a list of names to represent all the daily newspapers. My chances therefore of actually going were quite slim, but provisionally I checked my jabs were in order and cancelled the week's appointments, hastily rearranging a surprise party for a friend. Within the hour my marching orders had come through; the Mail and the Mirror had been selected and I should turn up with my passport at the MOD in Whitehall before the end of office hours to receive my Saudi visa.

In late 1990 entry visas to the desert kingdom were at a premium. With all applications carefully scrutinised and entry restricted mostly to a maximum of a month, by Christmas few newspapers had correspondents inside the country despite the deadline to war ticking away. Conscious that my passport was unlikely to be looked at by Saudi immigration because I should be travelling on a military flight, visa number 006638 assumed the journalistic equivalent of the Crown Jewels.

As I packed that night the prospect of a flight home on Christmas Eve seemed remote and I absently folded in a few extra shirts. I had been to the Gulf before, in fact only eighteen months earlier, accompanying the Waleses on a tour, and had been a guest at a reception in one of the Emir of Kuwait's sumptuous palaces by now, no doubt, trashed by the Iraqis. Smith though, a friend for many years, had been out much more recently enduring the heat and the frustration of the early days of the crisis in Jordan and he had a kind of fascinated loathing for the place.

The lumbering Tristar we boarded late that afternoon December 20 after many hours delay resembled a flying warehouse. Most of the seats had been stripped out and crates of spares for mechanised warfare were lashed to a floor dominated by huge turbine engines for one of the RAF fighter wings. It promised to be a noisy and uncomfortable flight and it didn't disappoint. There were, of course, no cabin staff and we were thrown a packet of squidgy sandwiches and fruit juice as we groped our way to our seats. Although the plane was largely given over to freight, the daily shuttle of supplies to the Gulf was fast reaching a climax, and there were a few passengers. Perhaps forty soldiers and airmen, some returning to units after compassionate leave, others carrying instructions to join unfamiliar regiments as part of the British build-up. One thing alone made them stand out from the men we had left on the ground — every one carried a gun.

Six and a half hours later, the Tristar began its bumpy descent over the pitch-black desert. Even at nightfall, the Saudi city exuded prosperity, wide lit streets with flashes of light reflected in the vast glass-fronted skyscrapers. Such is the wealth of this country the cities are virtually rebuilt every ten years. There was one snag though, as we taxied to a halt. This was not Dhahran but the Saudi capital Riyadh. This was the start of what was to become a familiar process, what the Army call "Hurry up to wait." We were ushered into a large dusty room of ugly, uncomfortable, tubular furniture when eventually our names were called out. We were assured that we would be on the next Hercules to Dhahran. "It would be a little basic, but we'll get you there," a smiling RAF man promised. When two hours later our names were not called for the flight there was a new duty officer. A flight was out of the question, the air force had more important people to transport than four journalists — the reporter and photographer from the Press Association made up the numbers. Even though we had travelled courtesy of the RAF and were sponsored by the MOD there was no shifting them. Now if soldiers are by necessity patient, journalists are anything but. Several raised voices later the RAF man agreed he would list us for the next flight at 10 p.m. that night. We were livid. At this rate there was every chance we would miss the Prince's visit in its entirety. It should be remembered that the days of journalists travelling with the royals were long over. Charles would be flying out the following day.

Both Ramsay and I realised we would have to make our own arrangements but feared compromising our unstamped passports. We had both been granted a one-month visa valid for three months and we hoped to protect this precious commodity by flying home with the military too. It would mean that as far as the Saudis were concerned we had never entered their country and our offices could send us back if the crisis hotted up.

In the warm early hours ground logistics crew were working non-stop and a friendly loadmaster who read the Mirror agreed to help driving us from the military airfield to the domestic terminal. We could have walked, but not only did we risk running into immigration but also the whole complex was swarming with armed troops. It was being shared by the French and British and while the quantity of matériel looked vast to us it was dwarfed by the American sector which was bristling with Cobra and Apache helicopter gunships. Under floodlights fighters were being armed and troops were marching up into the back of waiting transporters.

After the frenetic activity outside, the spotless marbled interior of the terminal was all cool calm. There were seats available on the first morning shuttle. We booked, and dozed for two hours till the flight was called. There was one more tricky moment when the police at the security check asked to see our papers. Ramsay and I had already decided not to present our passports claiming that we were only making a day trip and had left them in our Riyadh hotel. Instead we proferred Metropolitan Police cards. Quite what they made of those they did not say and anyway they were more interested in my shoes which kept tripping off an electronic alarm and they made me pass them down the conveyor belt to be scanned three times before they were satisfied (it turned out my black loafers were filled with nails).

From the air, Dhahran looked what it was before Saddam's invasion, the oil capital of Arabia. Refineries were spread out on the desert floor while on the Gulf huge tankers jostled with small dhows, a reminder of an older prosperity. But as the jet nosed down sights of another kind came into view, the hardware of a military defence. And on three sides at least, mile upon mile of sand as far as the eye could see.

The formalities were swift and painless and within moments we were bundled by a toothless old Bedouin in a grubby dishadash into a yellow Chevrolet of the kind seen on the streets of New York. "Which hotel you want?" he asked as we lurched off and before we could answer he stumbled on in halting English, "not International

5

Hotel, very bad." "Why?" we asked. "Because its near airport and base, fuel everywhere, big target for Saddam — ha ha ha." We booked into the Meridian, a 20 minute drive away on what Dhahran calls its corniche. But after checking in we returned almost immediately to the International which was where the British and Americans had established their joint information bureau and from where the Saudis issued their accreditation passes.

Now getting accredited is one of those most tiresome details of a reporter's life, and quite often the most useless. Nonetheless, we patiently filled out the Saudi' forms, explaining purpose of visit, duration of stay and, after queueing at various desks, were pleasantly assured our passes would be ready the following day. They were, and quite honestly for the next month, I don't think a single person looked at them. The airless first floor of the International's conference room was like a series of mini fiefdoms. There were the Saudis, their desks split between immigration — remembering my unstamped passport I made a mental note to avoid them at all times — and a permanently absentee military one — an aggressive group of exiled Kuwaitis, and an efficient US setup — boasting maps, data and twenty-four hour service, side by side with a curious British arrangement. An enquiry at the American desk usually brought someone snapping to attention, but the British treated us to a withering 'why are you disturbing us?' look, and the helpful answer, 'have you tried the MOD in London?' Since we were 3000 miles from London this was to become a source of increasing irritation. The Joint Information Bureau, or JIB as it was shortened, was the centre of all journalistic activity. After Iraq had marched into Kuwait the previous August newspapers all over the world began dispatching correspondents and television crews arrived by the jumbo load. On the map Dhahran, 150 miles from the Kuwaiti border looked closest to the action. It was here the US and British airforces had based the first of their fighter squadrons and because of the influx of journalists, the Saudis reluctantly set about instigating an information system. By the time of my arrival more than 1600 reporters, photographers, cameramen and technicians had been processed. I was number 1645.

But in the week before Christmas, with many correspondents having been ejected because their visas had expired and others taking a strategic chance by flying home for the holiday, the town was strangely quiet. There was a small crowd in the JIB that morning and I looked around to see if there were any faces and inevitably there were. Some were familiar. Paul Maurice, a former colleague at the *Mail*, now with IRN, Chris Buckland of the *Daily Express*, a delightful and amusing man who could illuminate any situation however grim, with a bon mot, and Patrick Bishop from the *Daily Telegraph*, an old friend from Belfast days. Another, an entertaining reporter from the *Independent* was Charles Richards was a new aquaintance. We were all to come to know each other well in the days ahead. Now even if I was marooned in a country that was like an executive nightmare — no mini-bar in the hotel room and no drink full stop — I was among good friends and, who knows the Prince of Wales could just provide us with some first class copy. If nothing else there should be some fun.

That night weather reports suggested that sand storms were brewing up in the desert and Charles's plans to visit the troops might be in jeopardy. Methodically, and with almost undue patience, we had been briefed on the Prince's two day programme by Lt. Col. David McDine, the head of Army PR in Dhahran. A tall, silver haired former newspaper executive, McDine was a territorial, one of the dozens of weekend soldiers who found there was a fine print in their part-time contract. He was also clearly able and extremely likeable. To my surprise he disclosed that Buckingham Palace had nominated me for what looked like the plum part of the tour — to be the only journalist to accompany the Prince when he visited the Type 22 frigate, HMS Brazen, remaining on board with Charles throughout the night. Suddenly the decision to send me to Saudi Arabia seemed terribly smart.

Dinner that night provided me with the first opportunity to sample Saudi cuisine in a restaurant decorated with photos of mountains — apparently donated by a Swiss Tourist Agency — called 'Vienna Woods'. It was a dismal experience as we were introduced to Saudi champagne, a sparkling, sweet and totally unfulfilling cocktail of fizzy water and apple juice. Meanwhile the first of Britain's promised 'second wave' of 15,000 troops, the 4th Armoured Brigade were arriving by Tristar from Hanover, Germany. Within a fortnight British military strength in the desert would have doubled.

It fell to their Commander, Brig. Christopher Hammerbeck, to put recent uneasy American claims that their troops were not ready for action into context. "If perhaps they are not as perfect as they wish to be they are nevertheless more perfect than the opposition." A remarkably prescient optimism that never faltered throughout the weeks and months to come. The remarks also symbolised a new mood of allied determination replacing the vacillation of the autumn.

Next morning, with refreshingly clear heads, Smith and I engaged a driver and air-conditioned limousine, and headed for the desert. Our rendezvous was Fadhly, a noisy and very popular service station about two hours along the shimmering ribbon of tarmac that cut through the desert north of Dhahran. It was packed with American servicemen who flocked to its supermarket to purchase the luxuries that made life in the desert a little more tolerable, chewing gum, cola, fresh fruit and soft lavatory paper. It was a modern day oasis, but of palm fringed water wells there were no sign. After purchasing bottles of mineral water ourselves we clambered onto the back of 14 ton Bedford trucks designed to carry ammunition, but today transporting the press. For 30 minutes we bumped and shuddered our way across the rutted sand in a spiralling cloud of dust. The old hands had shemaghs, the Arab head-dress, around their faces, while we spluttered into handkies. Our destination was a remote clearing where 56 Challenger tanks of the Queens Royal Irish Hussars were shrouded in their desert disguise between folds in the sand.

The Irish Hussars are one of the British Army's most distinguished cavalry regiments, direct descendants of the Light Brigade with 305 years of unblemished history behind them and 108 battle honours from Balaclava to El Alamein. Winston Churchill had been a subaltern with them during four years service in India, and their motto 'Might and Main' was just as important to the 654 men of the regiment today. Prince Philip was their Colonel in Chief, but their Commanding Officer was the dashing Lt. Col. Arthur Denaro, a colourful fair haired man, richly tanned by ten weeks in the desert and with all the elegance of an Army officer from the old school. A competent polo player he had brought to the Gulf as a memento a family heirloom — a silver cornet with which he liked to startle the camels. The Prince of Wales was due any moment and a frisson of excitement ran through the photographers, who had not had a decent photo opportunity for weeks. Poor Charles has

8

had to yield to all sorts of cheap shots for cameras over the years once grimacing to me: "We're not performing animals you know." On another memorable occasion, wincing after a string of "Hey, Prince" calls, he remarked: "Makes me sound like a bloody Alsatian."

But as we waited in the heat I knew this was one performance he would not want to miss. Roaring across the sands at the command of a mighty Challenger called Churchill. For Charles, a passionately peaceful man, who hoped above all that the crisis could be resolved without the use of force, it was nonetheless a unique opportunity to affirm the battle readiness of the British forces. What he had seen filled him with both pride and confidence. "It was a miracle of organisation," he said. But he was cautious too. "Of course anyone would be worried about what might happen but what has come across to me is that morale is marvellous." Sand encrusted his uniform of the Royal Iniskillen Dragoon Guards and as he brushed himself down he was asked if he had actually driven the tank. "No," he said "but at least I managed to get on and off it without breaking my arm!"

It was a typical Royal visit — a few rapid moments of handshaking and muttered greetings and he was off, this time by helicopter to visit another tank regiment, the Royal Scots Dragoon Guards, whose pipes serenaded the Prince with The Green Hills of Tyrol and The Scottish Soldier. On a day of blistering heat and with sand being churned up by the snarling Challengers, the sound of bagpipes was an enthralling interlude. A Puma whisked the Prince from the desert to the shores of the Gulf in a few minutes, while the rest of us clambered back aboard the dusty trucks for the bone shaking journey by road. As I emptied my shoes of Arabian sand for the umpteenth time I cursed not packing any boots, but then reasoned it was hardly worth it for one solitary visit to the desert.

At Al Jubail the army deposited me on the quayside and after Charles had been piped aboard I dashed up the gangplank behind him. I had been told I would need "appropriate dress" so all day I had been lugging around a change of clothes, including jacket and tie for, I assumed, dinner in the wardroom. Now the Royal Navy had been playing a role every bit as important as the Army and Air Force in Operation Desert Shield, but somehow it didn't have the

9

same impact. With a journalist captive for the evening, HMS Brazen were determined to reverse that trend. But at 6.pm. that Saturday evening, my only concern was filing a report on Charles's day in the desert to the Mail's sister Sunday paper. I had in advance been cleared to use the ship's Marisat satellite communication equipment, provided I paid at the commercial rate. I readily agreed and for twenty painful minutes dictated my copy down a crackling line. But considering we were steaming at 13 knots 60 miles out to sea, it was a marvellous feeling and £200 well spent. Later I caught up with the Prince as he toured the ship's company. It was an enthusiastic trip, up ladders and down narrow companion ways taking in a real Chinese laundry and tea with the Petty Officers. Armed with four Exocets and two six-tube Sea Wolf missiles systems, Brazen was bristling with defence, but like the troops who sat and waited in the desert her orders were of mind-numbing tedium, criss-crossing a section of the gulf on the same co-ordinates day after day, seeking contact with freighters trying to bust the trade embargo on Iraq. Those that did were either remarkably stupid — the Gulf was the most militarily congested stretch of water in the world — or driven by the highest misplaced ideals.

For a civilian a fighting ship is full of surprises, like the lack of doors to the washroom showers and the description of toilets as 'heads'. But there was another surprise in store. Having been invited as pool man to join the ship I reasonably expected to be sitting down with the Prince and the rest of the ship's company of officers for dinner. Not a bit of it. I did eat in the wardroom, but it was off my knees and at double quick time before it was the Prince's turn to dine. This seemed a great opportunity lost, but I shouldn't really have been surprised. The relationship between Press and Royal Family had disintegrated so much in recent years it was in reality little more than attrition. When I remarked about it later I was told: "Christ, if you'd been there you'd have given the Prince indigestion." I did learn though, that Charles was relaxed enough to quote one of his more feeble jokes adapted for the Gulf. The one that goes: "I hear that American soldiers here are queueing up for vasectomies — because it is such a snip."

That night the wardroom dinner was salmon mousse, chicken in lemon, and fresh fruit salad, washed down by red and white wines. It was this type of cuisine alone that infuriated the soldiers in the desert, who had already been living on compo rations for more than two months. To be fair though, the mess bar was generally locked up, though later I did spend several convivial hours there in the company of the ship's doctor and the Prince's private secretary and bodyguard.

Next morning, dyspeptic and a little tired, I was roused at dawn to see Brazen steam back to Jubail port. Prince, valet, bodyguard and reporter were deposited on the dock and a convoy of cars hustled us down the road at breakneck speed to the next engagement. Being driven in official convoys is great fun. It always reminds me of how the Commissars of old Eastern Europe travelled with citizens leaping for their lives as official cars sped by with total disrespect for any other road or even pavement user.

The RAF were the first arm of the military scrambled to Gulf duty. Bronzed and handsome the top class pilots have been in the desert for 4 months. At RAF Dhahran there were 18 Tornado F3 fighters which had been christened the Desert Eagles. They were in reality two merged Squadrons, the 29th and the 43rd. Charles incidentally, now in the uniform of a Group Captain, flew Phantoms with 29 Squadron himself in the early 1970s. Armed with Skyflash and Sidewinder missiles the Tornados were to play a decisive part in the battle to liberate Kuwait. As he toured the base the Prince came across a project after his own heart. A low rise, low cost, vernacular building constructed from local materials in which people could gather together as a community — an air raid shelter. Albeit of primitive beauty, sand filled hessian bags, it was according to the men of 53 Field Squadron, 39 Engineering Regiment, the state of the art in Saudi Arabia. The crudely constructed American imitations were simply 'no contest' the Prince was told. The Sappers, like all the British forces, he said, were facing war in the absence of their families at Christmas, with stoicism.

Charles was flying home and back at the Meridian there were two messages. One was confirmation of my flight by KLM to Amsterdam, locator number R7H 3NL, the other an urgent call from London. It was Peter Birkett — would I mind awfully staying on a bit longer? The Editor wants someone in theatre over Christmas — perhaps up to the New Year. It was not unexpected. Suddenly out of Washington that night the signals which had been so cloudy for the past few weeks cleared. Bush was saying he could go to war in ten minutes, and General Schwarzkopf, 'Stormin Norman', was warning the troops to prepare for a sneak Christmas Day attack by the Iraqis.

The following day, Christmas Eve, our numbers by now even more depleted, Ramsay and the Press Association had flown out on the heels of Prince Charles, Chris Buckland and I drove to Jubail to watch the 67th Ordnance Company unload presents and greetings cards for the troops. Back in November commanders complained that the British public were not behind 'our boys'. The response was extraordinary. Tens of thousands of parcels and letters arrived using the BFPO 3000 post code and addressed simply to 'A Soldier', A Sailor ' or 'An Airman'. There was crate upon crate of what the Army call 'Welfare Goods', perhaps 100 tons in all. They came from cigarette companies, board game manufacturers, toiletry firms and magazine publishers. There were mince pies and christmas puddings, Mr. Kipling had been exceedingly generous. In addition, for every single soldier, a gift pack from the British Legion. They weren't in truth terribly exciting. Inside each white box was a greeting card, pocket torch, toothpaste, talcum powder, a frisby and a beer token valid until 1992. But mostly the gifts were from private citizens. The fact that good natured, generous and kind people took the time and trouble to sit down and write words of friendship to men and women quite unknown to them, struck the troops as evidence of an essential goodness in British life. One soldier alone proudly showed us 90 letters from complete strangers, schoolchildren, housewives and pensioners.

With Christmas Day traditionally a slow news day — normally I would expect my report of the Royal Family's church service and the Queen's Speech to be the main event — turkey and plum pudding with the troops in the front line looked like very good copy indeed. I had hired a four wheeled drive truck and Chris and I set off for the desert at 5 a.m. At Fadhly we joined up with the TV crews, headed by Martin Bell of the BBC and Paul Davis of ITN. A military escort was on hand to rendezvous us with Brigadier Patrick Cordingley, the urbane commander of 7th Brigade. A friendly outgoing man who had won immense respect from his men, his charm belied an inner steeliness. Despite two torpid months in the desert his enthusiasm for his task remained undimmed. The paradox of the occasion, men of war singing carols about peace, was not lost on either of us.

Thanks to the extraordinary foresight of Paul Maurice, Christmas night did not turn out to be quite as ghastly as it could have. As I tried to find the enthusiasm to enjoy a cheese omelette in the hotel coffee shop, he conspiratorially invited me up to his room. Inside he hurled an army issue water bottle into my hand. Undiluted, mature Scotch — and together with Pat Bishop and Charles Richards we polished it off.

If Christmas Day had altogether seemed slightly absurd, then Lt. Gen. Sir Peter de la Billiére used Boxing Day to reinforce the 'war at any time' theme. Sir Peter, known as 'piano wire Pete' after his exploits as commander of the SAS, was the head of all British forces in the Gulf and Britain's most decorated soldier. Just to underline his upbeat battle readiness, still a sharp contrast from the more cautious Pentagon which believed President Bush was rushing into a desert Vietnam, Royal Marines stormed a ship carrying banned cargo for Iraq in the Gulf.

It was at a chance remark from the General that Saddam, who had been set a deadline of January 15th to remove his forces from Kuwait by the United Nations and had showed no intention of doing so, that I called London for clearance to wander around the border. Such a trip would not normally need executive approval, but if caught there was every chance that the Saudis would sieze my accreditation, or worse still, deport me. It was 3 hours hard driving from Dhahran and would doubtless mean check points. On moderately dangerous assignments Fleet Street competition can almost diminish so Buckland, Bishop, Richards and I levered ourselves from our beds at dawn to travel together. We were after all, the only newspaper correspondents in the country and there seemed a comfort in numbers. It may have been our pale skin but we were waved through the only Saudi check point en route and sped on to the border town of Khafji, where we had a remarkable slice of luck. We had stopped at what we took to be an American observation post but the soldiers turned out to be Saudis. A young officer, eager to practice his English, introduced himself as Awad, a 29 year old lieutenant. We asked if he would escort us to the border and only too happy to please, he bundled us into his jeep for the ten minute drive. There from the roof of a command post that looked like a legion-

13

naires fort out of 'Beau Geste' we could watch the Iraqis half a mile away, across a no-mans-land of scrub and sand, and as we stared through powerful binoculars, Awad told us far from pulling out, Saddam's men were digging in, fashioning tank traps and fox holes. Throughout the night they had noticed a stream of reinforcements and on an icy day — winter finally arrived in the desert on December 27 — the menace of these troops massing almost within earshot, was not lost on us. An open ditch and rusty chain link fence marked the border. It would perhaps take ten minutes to walk across the flat sands to reach the Iraqis who appeared to have made their headquarters in a commandeered coast guard station.

Awad had some parting words for us: "Tell them Saddam's troops aren't going — they are still arriving." At a US intelligence briefing that night, back in Dhahran, the Americans finally conceded that Saddam's intention was to remain in Kuwait "for the long haul". Iraq's might was estimated at half a million troops, 4,000 tanks, 2,500 armoured personnel carriers, 2,700 artillery pieces and 700 combat aircraft, all dug in, we were told, by the most imaginative defensive construction since the Siegfried Line. Conflict was getting ominously close.

War literally seemed in the air on December 28 on a routine visit to meet the men of an RAF helicopter support squadron at Razalga. As I was about to board a Puma an alarm blared out across the airbase. Iraq had launched a Scud, only the fifth since the Gulf crisis began but the third this month. Such was the ability of allied satellites and the Awacs early warning radar, the missile had been pinpointed in its pre-launch countdown, but no one was taking any chances. The status was 'yellow alert' and that meant NBC suits. For those of us, like this correspondent, who had forgotten their kit, it was a moment of supreme embarrassment, and some nervousness. Like misbehaving schoolboys, BBC reporter Martin Bell and I and a few others, were grouped into an airtight chamber as we anxiously waited for news of the missile's progress. Twenty minutes later came the all clear. The Scud had landed harmlessly inside Iraq but provocatively it had been fired from west to east, in the direction of Israel, a sign of things to come. But it was our unpreparedness that infuriated the army. From now on they decreed, no one without NBC kit would be allowed to join facility trips. Not only that, intense training was to start at New Year.

The signals from the Mail in London meanwhile, were clearing too. With no sign of success in gaining a visa for our chief reporter and Gulf expert, I was to remain in Saudi Arabia and probably for the duration of any conflict. Although it was unquestionably a great journalistic story, there didn't seem to be much to celebrate on New Year's Eve, which was just as well for Dhahran is not noted for its night life. Charles, Patrick, Chris and I booked a table at the Galaxy Indian Restaurant. We needn't have bothered, we were the only guests, and by 10 p.m. the vacuum cleaner was out to encourage us to leave. For the first time in years, none of us was up for the New Year.

On a shirt sleeved New Year's morning, Major Bob Fanshawe, was demonstrating how to administer morphine for serious injury. It is important, he was saying, to write an 'M' on the forehead of the victim together with the time and date of the injection. "We do this because in the Falklands there were lots of cases of morphine over-doses," he explained. Sitting on the sports field at the back of the International Hotel with overweight American correspondents shuffling around a running track behind us the situation had, not for the first time, a touch of the absurd. Major Fanshawe was one of the more agreeable figures in the army's public relations set up, not least for the wide-brimmed Boy Scout hat he wore, actually a result of his two year attachment to the Australian army. We had christened him 'Major Disaster' because of his uncanny ability to get lost so spec-tacularly. A few days earlier, after volunteering to run a colleague to a military base a few miles out of town, the two spent more than 3 hours driving in circles through the desert. My friend missed his plane and Bob learned some interesting new words.

Officially the British did not require correspondents to be fit, but Major Bob, a Royal Marine, began exercise classes which were not over subscribed. Some reasoned that they weren't worth going to because Bob would have got lost leaving his room. The Americans on the other hand, were making basic fitness an absolute require-ment for journalists who wished to spend time with their front line combat troops on manoeuvres. There were sit-ups, push-ups and a two mile run to be completed in under twenty minutes. I do not believe anyone failed — indeed one reporter was so fit his glowing details — 81 push ups, 96 sit ups and 2 miles in 12.59 minutes — were pinned up to encourage the rest. He was naturally a repre-sentative of the service paper 'Stars and Stripes'.

It is hard to imagine the Archbishop of Canterbury employing secret police to go round Britain terrorising people for not behaving in a Christian manner but that is exactly what happens in Saudi Arabia. We had been pretty much untouched by local customs until our brush with the Muttawa, a sinister force whose job is to uphold Muslim law on behalf of the Orwellian-like Committee for Encouraging Virtue and Discouraging Vice. Their number and the nature of their duties, are obscured by tradition and an obsessive secrecy. They say they are answerable only to God and their powers seem unlimited as we discovered. I was dining with a female correspondent in a Dhahran restaurant when an altercation broke out in the doorway. A young Arab man with wild eyes was pointing and screaming in our direction. He marched up to the table and demanded that the 'infidels' — us apparently — leave. My colleague, who was not only smoking and wearing long trousers, seditious enough, but flouting the law by eating in a restaurant to which women were not permitted. We had forgotten that women were only allowed in specially designated family restaurants provided they sit behind a screen. There seemed little point in arguing — we would jeopardise the living of the Indian proprietor. And as gracefully as possible under the circumstances, we left. It was, we later agreed, nice to know what freedoms our troops were defending here. Such was the zealousness of the Muttawa they had recently raided a local hotel which was enjoying a European food presentation. Upending tables on the way, they made for a stack of Swiss cheeses, into which the national red cross flag had been stuck. Siezing the offending emblems they went on their way. So careful were the allies not to upset Saudi sensibilities our war time hospitals had to be marked with the politically acceptable Red Crescent.

The world-wide coalition to expel Saddam meanwhile was coming on apace. The Grand Alliance of America, Britain and France now embraced 28 nations, including some of the most bankrupt on earth, from Honduras to Bangladesh, Senegal to Pakistan. There was even a detachment of 480 troops from the African republic of Niger, whose duties took them not to the front, but to the Muslim shrines of Medina and Mecca. And the Mujahaddin guerillas of Afghanistan got in on the act, sent to advise on Soviet weapons which the Iraqis possess. Such a global response to the crises reflected the new world order. Russians, Czechs, even Bulgarian forces had responded. Until the fall of the Berlin Wall Britain could never have countenanced removing half her military strength from Germany to another theatre. America too had denuded her European forces. Had the Soviet Union the inclination, Russian tanks could have been at the Channel ports within days. Saddam never grasped that such an alliance was possible because of the crumbling of the old way in Europe. But if there was disappointment in the role of Japan and newly united Germany, military commanders in Riyadh were only too happy to disclose how many Sony Walkmans had been despatched from Tokyo to the boys at the front.

On January 3rd armies that had been sent to defend Saudi Arabia now looked capable to not just repel an invasion but to launch one. Certainly back in August and perhaps only six weeks ago, if Saddam had pushed south he could by now have fulfilled his dream of being Emperor of Arabia. At the moment though he was content to plunder Kuwait and launch rhetoric at the Allies. The 'Mother of all Battles', he promised. Kuwait would become a cemetery with no tombstone for aggressors. Hyperbole was to remain a feature of the crisis but between the invective the Allies had amassed an extraordinary presence from a stranglehold of warships which stretched from the Eastern Mediterranean through the Red Sea and Indian Ocean and into the Gulf itself to 1750 airplanes, and an army of almost 600,000. Just to appreciate the sheer scale of it I took a drive towards the border under a blood red sky. Where a week ago the dual carriageway that heads north was silent, camouflaged tents had sprung up like flowers in the desert after rain. Vast equipment parks as far as the eye could see: Challengers, the American M1A1 tanks and Abrams fighting vehicles, British Warrior personnel carriers together with the machinery of attack, bridge building trucks and obstacle clearing vehicles. British troops, still arriving, were spending barely 24 hours at Black Adder lines, the receiving station, named after the television series, before motoring on to their front line positions and desert training. On January 4th Iraq ominously sent another 20,000 young men to the front. A few media reinforcements were also on the way. Those who had preserved their visas were flying back to Saudi from Britain with back-packs full of survival kit, Arctic sleeping bag, bivouac, thermal underwear, and army style webbing belts. Just for a moment our grip on reality seemed to slip. Did we really think that perhaps up to 2000 correspondents would be allowed to roam the desert in hot pursuit of the Allied troops? Nonetheless it was a great excuse to go shopping.

Saudis are not known for their love of camping, but eventually Chris Buckland and I did manage to each get our hands on a flimsy sleeping bag, an orange lilo, and some rather nasty polyester thermals. If nothing else it made us feel much more important lugging it around. The Americans had already set up their combat reporting system whereby correspondents would pool their despatches. Pat Bishop and I had been nominated for the two overseas spots for the Marines and US Army but we were more anxious the MOD seemed to be dragging its feet over its arrangements. Since the Falklands War when military and media clashed frequently and openly so much that it led to a Parliamentary enquiry, relations between Whitehall and journalists had been one of simmering hostility. Some of the reasons are obvious — the military's need for secrecy for example, and the journalist's permanent desire for openness. But there are other more complex differences. While soldiers are used to a tight, disciplined, heirarchical organisation, reporters are from an independent, freewheeling, competitive environment. Commanders were on the one hand suspicious of the different set of impulses which motivated journalists, while on the other recognising that they were a part of the war effort in maintaining public support. Access though was the key. It would give the military the control they desired. So because there were so many journalists wanting to cover the war — by now the MOD in London was finally sponsoring visa applications — both Whitehall and the Pentagon adopted similar pooling arrangements.

That night, January 4th, Lt. Col. Nick Southwood, head of public relations, in Saudi, proposed pools attached to the Army, Navy and Airforce, with a balance between tabloid, broadsheet, TV and radio. All the material could be used by any outlet so everyone would have access to the same information. It may seem an equitable approach but in the highly competitive world of journalism it is anything but. It provoked a short, bloodless, but vicious war. Everyone wanted their man, or in one case, woman, at the front. Known as 'mobile reporting teams', or MRTs, the only two that mattered were the seven man groups attached to the 7th and 4th armoured brigades. Behind them, and attached to the first armoured divisional headquarters, was the FTU, or forward transmission unit, primarily for television and radio with their satellites for sending back their reports, as well as those from the brigades. Further back still were the airforce MRTs attached to RAF squadrons in Dhahran, Tabuk and Bahrain. Finally at sea a solitary naval MRT with the ships of the Royal Navy. For the ministry it was more than enough but for the media it wasn't half enough, and battle commenced, ricochetting from Dhahran to London and back to Riyadh. The big guns of the BBC and ITN snuffed out the claims of Sky and TV am and then set about arguing among themselves. Fighting among newspapers was as ferocious as that of pit bull terriers. We print reporters, dubbed 'the pencils' by the army, offered a few modest proposals but with a large mixture of insouciance. Whatever happened would be decided in London and was beyond our influence.

For a fortnight I had had a request in to visit the most forward British army position, and on January 5th finally got clearance to meet the men of the Queen's Dragoon Guards, hidden away on a spit of land near to the Kuwait border. As you would expect, the natural inheritors of the famous long range desert group were not easy to find, but they had relayed some rather unmilitary jargon. "Watch out for the plastic spoons," they told us. And sure enough, firmly driven into the sands, the spoons led us to their encampment spread across the Gulf shoreline. A reconnaissance group, theirs would be one of the most dangerous if war came, operating behind enemy lines to disrupt the Iraqis second defensive screen. There was no doubting the resolve of these Welshmen — 60% of them were recruited from Cardiff and the valleys — as 28 year old Corporal Andy Milton told me. "If we let Saddam go now we will be back in three years to do it all over again. By then there will be nuclear missiles pointing at us from Baghdad." And this from a young man who knew all about warfare and every reason to fear it. In 1982 he had been a private in the Welsh Guards when Argentine rockets turned the troop ship 'Sir Galahad' into an inferno, claiming 39 lives. Every stitch of his clothing was burned to a cinder, but he survived that Falklands experience, only to find himself at the sharp end of another confrontation. Next day, with peace hopes withering on another strategic burst of rhetoric from Baghdad, the newly arrived Brigadier Hammerbeck was making further perceptive judgment: "My guess is that presented with the sort of attack that is going to come against them (the Iraqi conscripts) both from the air and on the ground, they may find it difficult to maintain their morale." Ultimately, he said, it was going to take the ground forces to throw Saddam out of Kuwait. Hammerbeck was clearly a man at ease in the limelight, and we wondered idly if there was now to be a 'rat race' between him and his opposite number with 7th Brigade, Patrick Cordingley. Brigadier Cordingley, who had had the publicity all his own way so far, snatched the initiative back on January 7th with the start of spectacular day and night manoeuvres with live firing that he promised would 'light up the sky like Blackpool illuminations'. Not for the first time I jotted down the word 'awesome' in my notebook.

In that second week of January the war seemed increasingly likely. Six Iraqi helicopters together with some of their most senior officers defected to Saudi, Middle East countries closed their air-space, and in Dhahran I discovered the first real casualty of war — room service. Like the rest of Saudi Arabia the restaurants, shops, petrol stations and hotels of Dhahran were all run by an immigrant workforce, and with no desire to be caught in the middle of a foreign war, they were fleeing home to the Phillippines, India and Bangladesh by every available 747. For the Arab citizens it was the moment of truth. They had remained indifferent to the influx of tens of thousands of foreign troops while civil defence sirens were blithely disregarded, but the realisation that they were losing their gardeners, domestic staff and drivers, suddenly jerked them awake. While the servants were offered huge bribes to stay, their masters were out buying up every conceivable piece of defence kit they could find, and a frenzy of panic buying and hoarding siezed the city.

Plans for the mass evacuation of the eastern cities of Damman, Jubail and Dhahran were rehearsed and air raid sirens sounded constantly. Typically though there was a display of stoical reserve from the ex-pat British community, 1800 at least employed by British Aerospace, and all vowing to remain to complete their con-tracts. At the British School the empty desks told a different story however. Of 290 pupils, 200 of them British, only 30 turned up for lessons on January 13 and just four teachers from a staff of 32. On that Sunday I called in to meet headmaster Geoff Fretwell, presid-ing over vacant classrooms, the school motto 'Let there be peace on earth' sounded strangely hollow.

On his final visit to the Gulf, Secretary of State James Baker, addressing American air crews warned that Saddam was a master of brinkmanship. It was clear that the dictator would wait until he was on the brink — the question was did he know when or where the brink was? Two days later I had cabled London — the Meridian was bursting at the seams with journalists and its telephone system could no longer cope — that the Americans would launch a massive air strike and bombing of strategic sites within 48 hours of the January 15 deadline. "January 17 — a moonless night — was seen as the perfect opportunity for such a strike," I wrote. It proved to be very prophetic. There was in turn a cable for me. London confirmed that I had been nominated for one of the pool positions with 4th Brigade.

DESERT WARRIOR

# DEADLINE

THOSE FINAL HOURS before the UN deadline expired were a blur of activity. There was a rush north to fulfill a facility trip alongside soldiers of the 16th/5th Queen's Royal Lancers — a good one as it turned out, for the troops were writing their final letters home before war between loading swing fire missiles and the 30 mm cannon of their Scimitar armoured cars. Lance Corporal Paul Earp was telling his parents back in Northampton that he knew what he was fighting for but he was a thoughtful young man who rightly worried about death – not his, but a friend's, "I don't think there are that many people who know how to deal with the death of a friend," he said. "The only thing you can do is not so much for them but for their families. If we ever get to meet their parents we can say 'I said a prayer for your son'. Touch wood I won't see any of my close mates die, but if they do I won't be telling anybody exactly how they died, I'll just say that it was quick. Maybe it will haunt us all for years to come, who knows."

When I got back to Dhahran I finally got round to opening a package of supplies London had shipped out via our political editor who had been shadowing the Prime Minister on his Gulf visit. There was the Gortex bivvy-bag, a sturdy Berghaus rucksack, sand goggles and a more comfortable pair of desert boots that I had dared hope. More equipment arrived that evening in the shape of a quilted anorak and some thick woollen socks. No one could tell us how long we were going for, although the original idea had been for a turn around of the MRTs every two weeks. Nor had we been told just what to provide. I telephoned the JIB and Colonel Chris Sexton, one of the Senior Information Officers, helpfully suggested washing and shaving kit, one towel, six pairs socks, four pairs underpants, three tee-shirts, one jumper, one waterproof, sewing kit, torch, mug, plate, knife fork and spoon, a lighter, some washing powder, clothes pegs and ear plugs. Oh, and a typewriter. It seemed the only item missing were cleft sticks. My first task on January 15th was to go to a local clinic for a blood test to determine my blood group, which the military wanted alongside my signature about next of kin. The managing editor of the Mail also called to assure me they had taken out a half-million pound insurance policy on my life. Camping in the desert was suddenly undergoing a slightly uneasy transformation. At the International the chosen few lined up for uniform and accreditation – yes more of that – as two RAF NCO's hunted through an untidy pile of desert kit for likely sizes. David McDine signed white MOD issue authority cards for a British war correspondent accompanying an operational force. Mine was No. 009. We also received shoulder flashes which confusingly bore the words 'Defence Correspondent'. At the same time we collected and signed for Annexe E. the media ground rules, which seemed on cursory examination fairly reasonable.

Within minutes I was dressed in combat jacket, trousers, scarf, and clutching a helmet and fragile looking camp-bed. There was time for a hair cut and to turn over my room to a Mail colleague, Geoffrey Levy, who had just arrived. Levy was fortunately on hand to ease my monstrous kit onto my shoulders. If we had any marching to do I was going to be in deep trouble. The rucksack was filled to overflowing, and the typewriter, the smallest I could find in Dhahran, seemed to have been hewn from cast iron. I had been instructed to report to Abu Hadriyah, a service station on the highway 100 miles north of Dhahran, where we would meet our escort officers and as there was no other way of getting there, I took a taxi. After heavy morning rain rags of silver cloud were spinning across the sky and white dust streamed off the salt pans as we drove through the desert. A taxi to the front seemed like another episode from 'Scoop' and reminded me of an earlier adventure. A few weeks before, Saudi Ministry of Information people had invited correspondents to spend a day at a dairy farm. A farm with green grass and herds of cattle in the middle of the desert seemed to good to be true. Like Evelyn Waugh's war correspondents they boarded a train for an unknown destination and when, after six hours, they had still not reached any farm there was a mild bout of panic that they had been duped into going because something was happening back at the front. At Abu Hadriyah there were introductions and farewells to make. I was met by Major Mike Gouldstone, a Ghurka, and the senior PR officer for 4th Brigade who introduced me to my escort officer, Captain David Irvine. This was the man who would make or break my time in the desert. I hoped we would get along.

The correspondents joining 7th Brigade, Martin Bell, Phil Jacobson of The Times, Mirror reporter Colin Wills and John Fullerton of Reuters were at the rendezvous too. Joining me were ITN's Paul Davies, together with his cameraman Nigel Thompson and sound recordist David McBride. I hurriedly purchased a cheap Arab blanket – I had no faith in that flimsy sleeping bag I'd bought – and we clambered into Japanese four wheel drives, suitably re-sprayed in desert uniform and set off.

The drive took us first north along the main road towards Kuwait and then for an hour east across the desert. At our first stop, 4th Brigade's administration area, I helped Irvine pull a sand coloured scrim net over the vehicle which cut out reflected glare from the wind screen. We had a date with the Brigadier, but he had moved on, perhaps to his headquarters. Before leaving Irvine stopped to re-move the fuses from headlamps, indicators and brake lights. Night driving was to become an unforgettable experience. Hunched over the wheel, peering into the darkness Irvine muttered: "You need the sense of a homing pigeon." It was not yet 6 p.m. but night had fallen like a great black curtain bringing with it an icy coldness. Like new boys at school, Paul, Nigel, David and I lined up for the evening meal. Tim Kelsey of the Independent on Sunday had joined us and over chicken casserole we were debating just when the UN deadline for Iraq to leave Kuwait would be passed. Midnight on the 15th — Eastern Standard time. Here it would be 8 am. on the 16th. We tell Major Gouldstone that we should like to interview troops as the deadline passes tomorrow. No problem, but in the meantime Briga-dier Hammerbeck wants to meet us. Tall, sandy haired and with 26 years in the army behind him I sensed that at 47 this was likely to be the high point of Hammerbeck's career. Why not? It was what he had trained for. His was the Royal Tank Regiment generally re-garded by army snobs as 'not very pukka' but he had been Brigade Commander for nine months. We were taken down a tarpaulin cor-ridor, formed of command vehicles reversed into an oval. In the map room we sat on benches as Hammerbeck outlined his philosophy: "I will tell you honestly what is going on because I want you to have the full picture and because I have the wives and families of my men, with whom you are the link, to think about. We are all on the same side. Now I intend to take everyone out of here alive, and because you have been put under my care, that includes you." It was a reassuring introduction but then he went on: "However, you have got to measure up to my standards. I am professional from the top of my head to the tips of my toes and in a very short space of time people could be firing at us. The teaching we are going to give you is to save your life." We should start he suggested, with some mental preparation. "I have been shot at before in Belfast," he said, " but my guess is that none of us here will have experienced what is likely to come." He let that sink in as he introduced us to the Brigade. Fifty nine Challenger tanks, 1,600 vehicles in all, which in a column end to end would extend 10 kilometres. And when the time came, Hammerbeck would be leading his men from the front. Ahead of us, perhaps no more than 50 miles away lay Iraq's fixed defence lines, minefields, anti-tank ditches and great sand obstacles. History, the Brigadier was saying, showed that linear applications did not survive the test of battle. Someone mentioned Saddam's experience gained from eight years of war with Iran. If Saddam thought the West would try and overrun him with human waves like the Iranians he was in for a shock. There were no stronger pacifists than soldiers and everyone, he said, had been secretly hoping there would be some accommodation so that Iraq could leave Kuwait with only hours to go. That did not look likely.

We drove back to the Brigade administrative area, the BAA. In the darkness a sentry challenged us. The British had copied the American two word password system adopted during Vietnam. It required a challenge from the sentry and a reply. Tonight it was "Picture – Tattoo". That first night in the desert I slept in an awning of Captain Irvine's tent, burrowing into my sleeping bag to read by torchlight, brought memories of boarding school flooding back.

*Jan 16*. We were woken at 6 am. It was still dark and Gunner Page, Captain Irvine's driver, put a bowl of cold water under my nose. Shaving was compulsory, the bristles can snag the respirator, halting its effectivess, he told me. As a fiery sun rose at 6.45 am.

our new home began to take shape. Beneath camouflage nets the camp was spread over a series of diamonds, ahead the cookhouse, beyond that the quartermaster's stores, and left the aerials of the signals truck. Further and to our right, another more isolated clump of antennae. "Out of bounds to you chaps," Major Gouldstone said breezily, "and don't talk to the soldiers there."

Some were walking past, tough and fitter looking than most of the headquarter's staff and we idly wondered if they were SAS. In fact I later learned they were intelligence, among them Arabic speakers monitoring Iraqi signals and briefed to interrogate prisoners. At 8 am. we were sitting around a transistor in the cookhouse which crackled into life with the World Service. The deadline for Saddam to remove his troops had just passed and, said the broadcaster, the world stood poised between war and peace. Among the soldiers there was a feeling of inevitability. Private Kendall Phillips paused over his baked beans, eggs and baconburger and said: "Does that mean we can get on with what we are out here for and then hurry home?" There was no answer but none was needed. His words were in the minds of all the troops here. But for the correspondents it was our first story. As I spooled paper through my Olivetti the irony of what was certain to be a high-tech war being reported by journalists using low-tech typewriters was not lost. In Dhahran I had left behind a laptop computer and satellite telephone, but this would be the first test of the Army's much vaunted copy run system. They had promised it would be 100-fold more efficient than that used in the Falklands, but then it had to be. It worked like this. After each reporter had finished typing the scripts were passed by our 'minders' to Mike Gouldstone, who drove back south across the desert to the Divisional Headquarters and the FTU. There the army operated its censorship post, and once cleared the copy was released for transmission. I learned later that in my first piece Hammerbeck's brigade strength had been struck out. Numbers of course fell within the ground rules, but in London, the Mail had written them back in.

There were more introductions to be made. Trench digging. On such a vast flat plain with no natural protection trenches offer the only sanctuary from attack. It takes about two hours to dig one six feet long and five feet deep and with a width that should be the span of the elbow to outstretched fingers. At 3 pm. klaxons sounded 'gas alert' and we scrambled into masks and NBC suits. The alert lasts for 40 minutes and it turns out to be a drill — perhaps for our benefit. Major Gouldstone who had watched our clumsy, pathetic attempts to put on our kit, orders intensive training. He also gives us a lesson in packing rucksacks and an idea on what we need — medical kit, insect cream, coil of string, dates or chocolate bar, torch with red filter, three; pairs of socks, t-shirt and underpants. "You should have a change of clothing — one on and one dirty," he says. After only 24 hours civilian life seems to be a memory.

That night orders came through to strike camp for an early move in the morning. Tents, camp beds and equipment was packed a way into vans and we slept on the desert floor.

# WAR

JAN 17. OPERATION DESERT STORM begins as US and British planes launch their attack on Baghdad at 2.32 am. Two hundred Tomahawk Cruise missiles fired from warships and submarines in the Gulf and Red Sea slam into command and control targets including the Presidential palace and Defence Ministry, while Stealth bombers, B52s and RAF Tornados join in. At 4.30 am we are roughly roused from sleep with the scream 'gas, gas, gas'. This time it is no exercise and the yell is as chilling as the night air. We were at NBC high — air raid red alert — masks, boots, and gloves. A colleague panicking after misplacing his respirator, begins to hyperventilate. I hide my fear in my trench while Gouldstone orders me to dig deeper. The emergency lasts an hour and despite the bitter cold when I pull my mask off my face is streaked with sweat and my inner clothes dripping wet. Sand has filled my lungs and pockets but the relief is tangible. We learn that the alarm had been triggered by the Cruise missiles — impacting on their targets. They had appeared to be Scuds on a bearing towards us. Someone brings out a short wave radio and a message from the Foreign Office to Britons in the Middle East is being relayed. It says: "Keep your heads down." From the soldiers there is an ironic cheer. In the past 24 hours we have passed two milestones — the first for Saddam to quit Kuwait, the second for the commencement of war. Hammerbeck says the start of hostilities is a signal for his men. "Now they know what the future course of events will be. It gives us a sense of purpose." It has also apparently knocked out Saddam's capability for launching a pre-emptive strike. Ironically as he speaks air raid warnings sound again. This time we can see and hear the reason. Two vapour trails on the horizon. Three huge explosions which shake the ground are all the alarm we need. Once again this is friendly fire — Royal Artillery rockets on a training exercise. It is a twitchy day.

On our way to watch infantry launch a mock battle we bump into the bulky figure of Lt. Col. Mike Vickery, the commanding officer of the 14th/20th King's Hussars. His squadrons of Challengers are 4th Brigade's cutting edge. Colonel Mike cuts quite an edge himself. A large, bulky figure with an elaborate shoulder holster and possesor of a sense of humour and fair play for which I am later to be most grateful. The exercise is by the Queen's Company of the Grenadier Guards whose standing orders that they must never be more than 24 hours from Buckingham Palace remain even in these days of jet travel.

Despite the allies air successes the routine continues on the ground. It does seem ironic though that just a few miles from this peninsula real battles are going on while we play war games. I squeeze into a Warrior troop carrier so full, I have to lie across the knees of the young guardsmen. When their moment to leave the vehicle to charge an imaginary trench position comes on the command 'de-bus' I am propelled through the open rear doors with the speed of an Exocet. When we get back to the BAA camp has been struck and the Brigade is on the move. We have also been joined by the photographer Mike Moore from Today and Simon Clifford a reporter from a local newspaper in the pool. Although from a rival publication, working as a team with Moore, I reason, will be good for both of us. There is nothing newspapers like more than pictures to go with words and vice versa.

The move is only a few miles but the Scud alarms do not let up. I have to type a despatch in full NBC kit in the back of a blacked out Land Rover. In the darkness, someone says we look like guardians at the gates of hell. Later sipping cans of San Miguel, a revolting alcohol free confection in Mike Gouldstone's tent, ITN want him to put a call through on Ptarmigan, the army's secure telephone line to the FTU. Afterwards I asked to speak to the man who is responsible for transmitting our copy. Another pool position, it had been won by an unlikely figure — the Financial Times political editor. Over the disembodied line come tales of woe — the fax blowing up — copy arriving late — copy not going out. Although disappointed I am not over surprised but when I relay this to Tim Kelsey he is appalled. He is horrified to learn that all his copy had gone first to the Daily Mail, not the Independent, but then since the Mail has offered to deal out everybody's copy when no one else would accept it, I can't see his complaint. Gouldstone's driver suddenly volunteers to motor us over to the FTU to find out at first hand what has happened. The visit confirms what I thought. Things are not so gloomy and I get to make a 90 second phone call to the office.

*Jan 18.* After getting used to finding our way round our last location we have to start all over again. So in the morning we follow the tinny sound of a radio. The transistor has become a central part of the culture of this war. Breakfast served between 7 and 7.30 is partnered by the World Service. News of allied air attacks are cheered but there is gloom at the loss of the first British Tornado. It is, I think, easy to be shocked by the calm exuded by these British soldiers, fighting for a country far from home, but there is about them a professionalism. They understand the issues of why they are here. What they want though, is to be allowed to get on with it. Already it seems that the talk of only a few days ago of heavy aerial bombardment followed by a swift and decisive invasion by the land forces is unrealistic. Just occasionally you catch a glimpse of returning bombers but their altitude is too high to identify them. It is the radio that tells us the largest air armada ever assembled is flying above us. There are two nasty breakfast time shocks — the first that we have to start taking NAPS — nerve agent pre-treatment — bitter white pills — one every 8 hours, because of growing fears of chemical attack. The other is that we are all to receive anthrax inoculations. No one can trust a man who has gassed his own people. At the dressing station attached to the Royal Artillery's 2nd Field Regiment, leg splints support the camouflage netting, cardboard lines the floor and a single 60 watt bulb is all the operating theatre is permitted. The doctor in charge of the unit, Captain Mark Paley, opens his rusty refrigerator, pushing aside cans of alcohol-free near-beer and cartons of cherry juice, and pulls out the anthrax vaccine. "You have to do the best you can. The British army has never fought wars where it wanted to," he says. Nearby the artillery is practising their M109 self propelled guns. The big Howitzers which last saw action during the Korean war work in batteries of eight hurling 106 lbs shells up to 12 miles. To the unfamiliar they are deafening beasts but their operators wear no ear defenders and gently mock those of us who cower with fingers in our ears. Colonel David Radcliffe, their commander who has the helpful manner of a provincial librarian, is certain they will be called into action. Recalling the bombing by air of Port Stanley's airfield during the Falklands War he says: "Everyone said 'hooray' at the time but it was another two weeks before we realised it had not been enough alone."

Saddam meanwhile has begun his retaliation, not against the infidel Allies nor even the kingdom of Saudi Arabia he so loathed, but the greater enemy, Israel. He launched the first of 40 Scud attacks on the Jewish state.

*Jan 19.* One of the most effective weapons the British brought to the Gulf was the multi-launch rocket system MLRS. Never before tested in combat, the rockets streaked across the sky with unerring accuracy at up to 20 miles. Each 4 metre long missile, delivering 644 separate bomblets was capable of being fired at the rate of one every 4 seconds. The Bengal Rocket troop of the 39th Heavy Regiment actually found a depression in the ground to demonstrate this new toy for us. Were we impressed? You bet we were. God knows how much it cost to actually detonate one of these rockets but Lt. Col. Peter Williams "call us the grid square removal service" actually fired off a whole salvo so Paul Davies could do his piece to camera with some action in the background. Davies, who won Television Reporter of the Year for his dramatic coverage of the Rumanian Revolution has a terrier-like competitive streak. Disappointed that he had not joined 7th Brigade where he had made many friends in the early days of the crisis, he and Nigel Thompson, who is newscaster Carol Barnes's husband, were determined to knock spots off the BBC. In Christopher Hammerbeck they found a commander who enjoyed being on camera as much as his men. The Brigadier was no doubt motivated in part by the desire to redress the balance in publicity terms in favour of 4th Brigade. I played no small part in this myself, and certainly by the end of the first week of war, 4th Brigade had the edge. With the arrival of Mike Moore it was to keep us firmly in the lead of the 'rat race'.

A visit to the 12th Air Defence Regiment was to see the Army's equivalent of a clay pigeon shoot. Over our heads Rapier missiles zig-zagged across a grey sky in pursuit of a drone, or tiny model aeroplane that acts as a target. The only difference from shooting down clays is that the missiles were not allowed to hit the drones. There are only four in country, and the idea was to let the missiles at £20,000 a time, pass nearby and explode on the horizon. In a few weeks time a whole bunch of Iraqis gave themselves up to one of these drones. And there never was any need to launch a Rapier or Javelin in anger because the skies remained the allies.

There are few women at the front but Lt. Karen Card was one of the exceptions. The 29 year old blonde administrative adjutant to the commander of the 39th Field Regiment I thought deserved praise indeed. I was discovering just how little privacy there is in the desert, but for a woman it must be doubly hard. It turned out the men dug her trench, and modestly screened off a shower area for her. We were still being assured that 3 inches of cold water was luxury but by coincidence water bowsers had delivered a fresh tank to the BAA and that night I enjoyed my first and last shower for a month.

*Jan 20.* Sunday and no dashing off to see other units, but reveille was still at 6 am. First thing in the morning Gouldstone could always catch one of us out without our respirators as we stumbled across the sand to the desert rose, an ingenious urinal, of up-ended mineral water bottles driven into the sand. This time though, he was the absent minded one. I think he must have been livid because for the next few mornings Gouldstone, who regularly stripped for an all over body wash, would stalk to the desert rose naked except for a respirator belted around his middle. The excursion to the latrines was another daily hazard. It was more or less out of bounds at night except in extreme cases, after rumours that Iraqi special forces were in the area. The very idea of meeting an unpleasant end in such an unpleasant place did ensure a queue every morning, and queue there really was. There was no room for modesty. A seat, a bucket lined with a bin liner and a hessian screen that came to hip height. But whatever time one went one thing was certain — the bag was always full. Motivation usually provided the concentration to change bags. The sound of burning shit was another unfamiliar one — it explodes. Along with other rubbish it was daily thrown into a deep gash pit, doused with petrol and set on fire.

I wanted to write a piece about the army that marches on its stomach, and in Corporal Alan Lewis and Lance Corporal Brian

Robertson, the Brigade chefs, I found two easy going companions. It was an inspired move. From now on I got five star treatment every meal time. Until joining the MRT it had been two or three years since I had eaten red meat but an army on the move is no place for vegetarians. In fact it was not the meat but the sheer quantity of food I found hard to take. A fried breakfast was followed on the dot of mid-day by a lunch of stew or casserole with fresh vegetables and apple pie or crumble with pink custard I hadn't seen since school days. Tea was at 4.30 pm, a curry perhaps. The evening meal was served early because no visible lights were allowed after dusk.

Mike Moore and I had asked to visit a field hospital. Dressing Station 5 Alpha was a few miles away across the desert and on the way we passed row upon row of Challengers, waiting for transporters to take them to the front. They were the Irish Hussars, part of 7th Brigade and not really our story but they made a very strong photograph and we persuaded Irvine to let us stop. The casualty unit looked at first like something out of the Crimea with its canvas tents and trestle tables but it was spotlessly efficient. There were four doctors, a Lt. Col., a Major and two women captains, and twenty medics. Additionally there were two dentists and seven clerical assistants, but it was the sixty Ghurkas who ran the field ambulance service that caught my eye. Perhaps the most ferocious soldiers in the British Army, they were as much as any one responsible for the Argentine surrender during the Falklands war. After serving with such distinction in the South Atlantic they eagerly anticipated being called up for the Gulf but this was to be an armoured infantry conflict and they only squeezed in as stretcher bearers. They had though, turned their ambulances into formidable machines. Sand bags lined the floor as a protection against mines, and no man was ever seen without his rifle.

Later Mike Gouldstone produced a miniature cross-bow. Small it may have been but the bolts were vicious indeed. With the kukuri at his waist and fluency in Malay and Nepalese and some Chinese, we had dubbed him 'Mad Mike' but in fact he was at 37 a desk bound Ghurka, attached full time to army public relations at South East district in Aldershot. Irvine, who gave Mike Moore and me a lesson in stripping down and using the SA80 rifle, on the other hand, was only on attachment as a minder.

Now at dawn the wet sand and churned landscape of slit trenches looked for all the world what it must have done on the Western Front during the Great War. At night those same trenches could be a death trap. On a copy run back from the FTU, ITN's minder, Captain Anthony Fairbanks-Weston, fell headlong into a trench, tearing ligaments so badly he had to be evacuated to hospital. Moore and I meanwhile were now alternating our sleeping arrangements so that every other night we could sleep in Irvine's tent. The other was spent under a sheet of the dimpled plastic sheeting that is called 'CARM' — chemical agent repellent material. Cocooned in sleeping bag and with a red filter on my torch it was just possible to write a bluey — the soldiers air mail letter form, and without telephones the only way of keeping in touch with home. Their delivery though varied, between 5 and 10 days. Writing to my foreign editor it struck me as extraordinary that in these days of satellite communications I should have to resort to the post and a delivery that was probably no speedier than that used by war correspondents 100 years ago.

Around 10 pm. there was a gas alert. We lay on our beds perspiring for about 3/4 of an hour. Somehow we didn't hear the all clear and Irvine summoned Gunner Page. Page, a 20 year old from Lincoln was not the Army's brightest recruit. Like a canary in a coalmine he had to remove his mask. It provoked the memorable response "Oh no sir, not the sniff test."

*Jan 21.* Iraq has launched Scuds into Saudi Arabia and the breakfast time banter is of the success of Patriot. Like Exocet during the Falklands, Scud has become the word of the war. We are to join the last live fire exercise by the tanks of the 14th/20th Hussars led by Brigadier Hammerbeck from the turret of his Challenger called 'Nomad'. Hammerbeck is still preaching caution. This war could last months and not weeks, he says. He is though, enjoying being photographed, pulling on gloves in an 'I mean business' routine and mentioned that he has heard from his wife. "I gather the Mail's coverage is a bit rich," he says. I don't know what he means but it is at least the first feedback.

The exercise which we pursue on top of a filthy tank recovery vehicle grinds on all day. There are long pauses when nothing seems to happen and I only wonder if it will be like this during the real thing. At dusk Giant Viper is detonated. It should be the high-light of the exercise and is the pride of the Royal Engineers mine clearing devices. One ton of explosives that snakes a destructive path through a minefield. It is though, very unreliable, and after leaping across the skyline like a demented firecracker, it just as quickly deflates. That night all of us are asked to decide which battle group we wished to join. Gouldstone has correctly identified that as correspondents we need to be with the fighting echelons if we are to get any flavour of war. That means breaking up the MRT and each joining different battle groups. 4th Brigade had 3 battle groups, one armour heavy, the 14/20th Hussars, and two infantry heavy, the Royal Scots and the Royal Regiment of Fusiliers. In a tank with driver, loader, gunner and commander, not a single place can be compromised and there is no room for a passenger. To join the 14th/20th would mean travelling with one of their support ech-elons, perhaps several miles to the rear. The infantry looks a far better, if more dangerous prospect. Travelling in a Warrior ar-moured personnel carrier we should be able to get out among the action. This is not bravado. It simply seems that having been pre-sented with the chance of covering a war well, then it is worth covering it properly. Both Paul Davies and I volunteer our names for the Fusiliers because an essentially English regiment promised to be the easier to deal with. Davies had compelling reasons — the Jocks would be hard to understand on TV. Gouldstone proposes that we toss and ITN wins. There is some natural justice in the world though — when he joined the Fusiliers, Paul found he had been placed with a company of Scotsmen.

*Jan 23.* Mike Moore, tall and easy going, had brought an infec-tious enthusiasm with him, not least because he and the other pho-tographers had had to wage a long campaign to persuade the Army to allow a cameraman at the front. He was excited about us joining the Royal Scots. As usual it took longer than it should. Irvine, who in my opinion, couldn't find his way out of a paper bag, continued to impress with his knowledge of map reading. We already have an uneasy feeling about how he is going to be able to deliver our mate-rial in the heat of battle. As we arrive the Royal Scots are holding an 'O' or orders group, cross legged in the sand. There are 22 officers and a kaleidoscope of accents. I suppose I had imagined that while the men would have thick Scots dialect, the officers would be pukka English. Not a bit of it — and the commander, Lieutenant Colonel Iain Johnstone has an added aggression and a direct rapid-fire delivery. It was the start of an exercise, but you would never have thought it. "I want to get the Jocks into the idea of stabbing and shooting," Johnstone was saying. "That is what the Jocks do best. It is good for the guys to let off some steam so I want them in those trenches killing Iraqis in a very big way." The ruddy-faced men, poring over the 'frago' the nickname for operational charts, were distinguished in one other way. Each of them was wrapped in body armour. Not only did it make them seem the most warrior like of all the soldiers we had met, it also gave us an extraordinary sense of security. Johnstone had one last oblique message to his men: "Please don't be rude to the Brigade staff." Hammerbeck and company were going to be monitoring their progress.

I join Major John Potter, B company commander, who has a fine line in self deprecation, and a nose burnished by the wind and sun to a scarlet hue. The troop carrying belly of the Warrior is like being packed in the family saloon on the car deck of a cross Channel ferry. It is not for the claustrophobic. For the next 30 hours we are battened down inside and because this had to be as realistic an exercise as possible, everyone was wearing NBC suits. The heat was stifling. As Potter's was the command vehicle there were racks of radio equipment which sent the temperature even higher and we were constantly bathed in sweat. The Warrior boasted a 30 mm Rarden cannon, up-armouring that would halt an RPG round, satellite navigation and — most important of all — the Bee-Vee. The boiling vessel, was kettle, cooker, oven, all rolled into one container and plugged into the vehicle's electric circuit. It meant that signaller Corporal Ben Gilchrist could provide a constant stream of instant coffee. While Potter commanded his company of infantry, anti tank, mortar and engineers, Gunner Jim Lee, known as 'the General', loaded and fired tungsten tipped armour piercing shells with frightening accuracy.

After six hours, Potter was ordered to clear a trench network. It was pitch dark and thick with cordite. There was almost wilful abandon as cannon, rifle and grenade detonated. "This is real live firing. Back in Germany we are lucky to get this much in a year," says the General. Potter wants me down low beside him, and I am only too happy to oblige. A couple of nights earlier, one of his colleagues, a Major, who headed the mortar section, had been shot three times while acting as a safety officer. Tonight the safety officers were marked with orange cylumes in their helmets and whistles between their teeth. Crouching beside Potter in the sand it seemed to me total confusion. The Army of course, call it the 'fog of war'. "Remember," said Potter "on the battlefield people get hyped up. They might not recognise you. They might shoot first. The adrenalin keeps pumping." I am not sure if he was grinning — it was too dark — but I resolved to make sure every single soldier in the battle group knew me in the days ahead. I started that very night by etching my name and blood group on my helmet like all the guys, and writing 'correspondent' in both English and Arabic on my tunic.

That night we lurched from objective to objective, sustained by coffee, corned beef sandwiches, tins of oatmeal blocks and an army favourite I remembered from school cadet days, biscuits, brown, broken.

*Jan 24.* The exercise was still continuing but I jumped vehicles so I could get across to regimental headquarters where Irvine was due to collect me. As I waited in the back of a mortar control vehicle for hours, as it turned out, I wrote a piece about these trench Warriors. The piece was later widely used by Scottish newspapers, and even Princess Anne, the Colonel in Chief of the Regiment, incorporated part of it into one of her speeches.

Collecting Mike, he was gushing about his night with A company. Back at base, the Brigade orders are to move in the morning. We have a new colleague too — Robert Fox of The Daily Telegraph. The training, it seems, is at last over.

This is what I sent to the Daily Mail.

There are a few moments in war when it seems better to be a soldier than a correspondent, but this is one of them. The infantry of the Royal Scots and the cavalry of the 14/20 Hussars in their tanks deployed across miles of empty sand must take for granted their part in the conflict that will surely begin.For those of us who little more than a week ago found ourselves pitched into service alongside the British build-up at the front, it has at times meant a conscious effort of will. Not only about transforming ourselves from, let's face it, a free, easy and in-dependent civilian life into a soldier's routine of orders obeyed, but also about coming to terms with our own confusion about what is ahead. How shall we cope with the fog of war? I hope we shall be permitted our apprehension.

For me these past ten days have been a revelation. While not in any way trying to diminish the role of the magnificent men who face long, hard and certainly bloody battles ahead, we too have had to undergo an intense self examination, a kind of battle preparation if you like. I suppose it was Brigadier Christopher Hammerbeck, commander of the 4th Armoured Brigade, who pulled it into sharp focus. On my arrival he looked me over in my newly-pressed pattern fatigues, a helmet hanging with the strap undone for all the world like Audie Murphy, and asked if I had thought through what was going to happen. Not to the troops, but to me. He didn't say it, but he was talking about death. About a 7.62 calibre bullet that comes out of the dark, or a mist of poisoned chemicals that dusts the ground like a deadly drop of spray. But surely, you think, as a reporter you are a mere observer? That impressive white identity card in your tunic pocket bearing your picture and the Ministry of Defence crest says war correspondent not soldier.

A week later in the dead hours before dawn, the realisation that there is no distinction, no room for mere spectators, begins to sink in. The air is alive with the sound of shrieking klaxons and the fearsome yell of "Gas!Gas!Gas!" And the Iraqi special forces, said to be at large in our area, will surely show no quarter with their piano wire and stealth. It is a comfort to think of the sentries at night in their foxholes, although how they dis-tinguish between friend and foe when every piece of desert brush takes on the form of a man I can only guess. For someone used to a daily newspaper office, where the lights of industry burn late into the night, life without so much as a candle is an extraordinary experience. There are, incidentally, enough perils in venturing out after nightfall in the shape of trenches, traps for the unwary, without worrying about Saddam's killer squads.

In a way these past days-and in the desert you have little con-cept of time or date-have been something of an initiation. One of our number has left already, ground down by routine as much as anything. Perhaps there will be others. In times of war, though, routine can be life preserving. So let me tell you about a day with the Desert Rats.

We rise each day at 6am when the flat half light looks as I imagine the Western Front did in World War 1. The sand is wet and clammy and in the gloom you can see heads moving about the parapets of the the guards' slit trenches. My home has been the alcove of a tent with a rickety old camp bed under sheets of pink CARM-chemical agent repellent material. In the days to come, I think I shall long for such primitive comforts. Washing over a basin dug out of the sand with a jug of cold water may not be the most dignified way of starting the day, but it does wake you up. In the cookhouse at seven, the World Service News is listened to intently by men who at home would rarely tune their transistor dials to Radio 4. The successes of Patriots in knocking out Scuds are greeted with cheers. The losses of aircraft acknowledged in silence. Scud has become the word of this war in the same terrifying way as the name Exocet filled every household with a sense of dread during the Falklands. In this build-up to battle, the day revolves around meals. We eat on our feet off disposable plastic while wearing full combat gear, helmets and flak jackets, ready to move in an instant. For all of us, the respirator that could be the difference between living or dying in a horrible way does not leave our sides. It hangs in its green pouch like a six-gun ready for the quickest of draws. We have a ditty about getting it on in under ten seconds: Be in time. Do it in nine. Stay alive and make it five.

Shoulders once familiar with nothing heavier than the cut of a gray flannel suit have grown used to a backpack that would do credit to a sherpa. And added to that are chemical-proof charcoal-lined smock and trousers, clumsy rubber over-shoes and water. We have been accustomed to the stages of alert for donning the gear. Just the other night I lay in my sleeping bag perspiring gently in the respirator for what seemed like hours as Scuds flew out of hearing above our heads. At a field casualty station, I lined up for an anthrax jab with our Scottish driver, Jock Johnson. "Better not turn us into badger," he said, suspicious of the needle. If Saddam had his way it could be the most vital unpleasant moment we ever have. To increase our resistance we are all taking NAPS-anti-nerve gas pills-washed down three times a day with stewed army tea. Morning can mean 'administration', the quaint army term for washing clothes, or if the water supply has got through, a cold shower. Being clean is just a distant memory. Sand permeates everything. Like the soldiers I have my hair shorn to the scalp. At night we turn our socks over the tops of our desert boots to keep out scorpions. Orders to strike camp come abruptly and must be followed swiftly. Camouflage netting is packed away and trenches over which we seemed to labour for so long, are filled in. That way we move on without showing sign of our presence. Driving is another unforgettable experience. At night it is like navigating in a blindfold. All the fuses must be removed from the lamps. In daylight, every halt has to be accompanied by throwing a 'scrim net' over the vehicle so that it melts into the sand. Night falls quickly like a great black curtain dropping across the skyline. By 8pm the camp is silent. Men are sleeping or alone with their thoughts. These hours are a time to reflect on the momentous days that lie ahead. What will it really be like? We have spent long hours with battle groups to give us the taste,sound and sight of war. But then no one was firing at us. To escape from these thoughts, I have burrowed under my sleeping bag to write 'blueys', the soldier's lifeline to family and friends and loved ones, by torchlight. It brings memories of boarding school flooding back.

There have been lighter moments in these past days. At first-aid class, my task was to heave Private Steve Smith, 16st and as solid as a rugby international, into a fireman's lift. He slammed over my shoulder with such force that we both hit the sand. Or the afternoon of rest recreation spent playing with a miniature crossbow when the correspondents proudly outgunned the army sharpshooters. They will be moments to treasure, faces to remember, to sharpen the mind when we are baptised by battle.

Now it is dark. Allied planes are rumbling overhead on their nightly run to Baghdad. The last week with the Desert Rats has been a privilege. The next few promise to be the most testing of their lives and certainly of mine.

*Jan 25.* Clearing up that morning was a curious affair. Paul Davies who seemed to get quite obsessive about washing, decided to rinse out some more clothes, while Robert managed to devote three whole hours to packing and unpacking his rucksack. Already there was apparent tension between Gouldstone and Fox. I didn't give much for the Major's chances — Robert possesses a cruel and quick tongue. They didn't tell us where we were going, only that we could change our date line from Eastern to Northern Saudi Arabia. It occurred to me that the front line stories I had been filing for the past ten days were thus not strictly accurate. The journey took us back to Abu Hadriyah where we spent 45 minutes eating our first meal off plates, but we tore the chicken apart with our fingers.

Under a diamond sky we journeyed in a convoy north. The road was empty of civilian traffic — just a steady stream of military vehicles. On hummocks in the sand, US MPs hunched over 50 calibre Brownings mounted on their ugly Humveys while helicopter gunships patrolled above. The whole 200 mile road was one long rolling replen. Heading north, lorries loaded with supplies. Returning south, empty trucks going back for more. By the time the brigade had completed its move some drivers had clocked 1200 miles. Both Mike and I took turns behind the wheel as we pressed on to the RP, 4th Brigade's receiving point, where heavy rain and heavier tracks had churned the sand to the consistency of glue. It was bitterly cold and we slept under sheets of CARM beside the vehicles, too tired even to dig trenches. Throughout the night, as the tanks and trucks ground by us, the sound of Allied bombers looking for Iraqi targets thundered overhead. It was an extraordinarily clear night and flashes of light flickered across the horizon. As I lay hugging the damp ground, the sound was like a sedative. Air support with its precision and power is everything — the cornerstone of all our hopes — and I found myself silently wishing the planes God-speed. With all this din of war around it looked as if both sides had committed themselves on such a scale that engagement would be inevitable.

*Jan 26.* There was no let up. At first light Chinooks began fluttering down to the desert disgorging infantry battalions who raced off to find track vehicles which had come on transporters by road. Watching the convoys inch past for hour after hour it seemed inconceivable that Iraq could match this gigantic logistical operation, that ensure nothing would be lacking, ammunition, fuel and spares on the day. We waited for orders to move most of the day. For a while I huddled in a MP's post for warmth and to read while the sentries directed the never-ending line of traffic. The ground and weather was harsher and it was late afternoon before we were ordered to move. Mike, I had long figured, must have been a good

Boy Scout, because he was so adept with camp poles, camouflage nets and tarpaulin. Irvine seemed to me useless and without Mike, he and Page couldn't put up an umbrella. Now I was no expert so I started to dig the first trench — not easy in ground like concrete — when Irvine barked at me to help with the tent. I bit my tongue, but I shall not much longer. The cookhouse served haggis — it was Burns night — and after dinner we took pickaxes to the stony soil. The sunset was a magnificent brick red but the wind blew the smell of rain across the vast plain.

*Jan 27.* The rain drove across the camp at 45 degrees battering the tent with such persistence it woke me before Captain Irvine could bellow 'NAPS' — our reminder to take those nasty little pills. NAPS were more or less untested and we all wondered what ghastly side effects they might have. Sexual for sure. No one could remember the last time he had felt aroused. It was too wet to dig, too wet to do anything. The wet and the cold would be an abiding memory of this war in the desert. ITN in a much smaller tent had almost been washed away and all Paul Davies' washing had been in vain. The planes we had heard last night had been B52s bombing Iraqi infantry. Attacks at night must surely be having a shattering effect on the Iraqis' morale. Yesterday's copy run to the FTU, we heard, had taken 17 hours — and that's before the shooting starts. I wondered if the Iraqi's had MRTs? Perhaps we should engage them with notebooks and films to the fore, flicking ink in their faces. Later we are reluctantly taken to a supplies area to meet Hammerbeck. Somehow the fact that 4th Brigade has only called in a fraction of the spares 7th Brigade needed in its first weeks in the desert seems a statistic of total insignificance. My first mail had arrived, a letter from David Williams, who had been with the RAF in Bahrain, and a parcel of goodies — fresh fruit and chocolate — from Steve Back in Dhahran. Our trench meanwhile had taken eight hours to dig. It was about as deep as a windbreak but the next day I found a rat dead in the bottom. A drowned rat. Looking around at the encampment there were an awful lot of drowned rats.

*Jan 28.* With so much kit wet and dirty, I get up to do some urgent washing. Suddenly, as though on cue, Captain Irvine says there is no time for that because we have to go — immediately. It seems a provocation too far. I suppose it has been bottling up inside me for some time and I fly off the handle on the lines of 'we're not soldiers, but civilians'. It is only a momentary outburst but the tension remains. Meanwhile it has been decided that we shall all return to our units where we will remain for most of the week. Mike and I have agreed that we shall both join the same company starting with A and then moving on to B before seeing which suits us best. Unfortunately Major Norman Soutar, A company commander, has an extra man in his Warrior and there is not room for both Mike and myself. I am placed with the second in command, Captain Bob Bruce, a languid Scotsman renowned for digging the biggest and the best crapper in the desert. Out here there is no luxury of latrines but a spade, a long walk, and a hole in the sand. Bob though, had got his section to dig an extraordinary affair, like a giant tomb, complete with steps, banisters and a toilet like a throne set on a plinth.

'A' company is arranged in a large diamond formation. To the front are the platoons on air defence duty, their camouflage nets pulled back to allow the Warriors machine guns and cannon to nose into the air. They offer a kind of protective screen all round the company. As part of my avowed plan to make sure all the Jocks know me before the shooting starts, we walk from Warrior to Warrior making introductions. Today there is only one word to describe the state of mind among the 170 men of the company — mellow. Not cool, not laid back, but mellow. It means much the same thing but it's what they say in the desert. Out here I am mellow some of the time but not all. I am certainly not mellow during a Scud alert when I am crouched in a trench breathing in lungfuls of sand and fear. Nor am I mellow when I think of the destruction a land battle will bring. And I am definitely not mellow when the soldiers talk about 'getting slotted'. That in the casual, throw away language of war, is what the soldiers mean by being killed. At least I think that's what they mean. The Americans call it 'being greased' but to the Jocks it's just 'getting slotted'. These are the men who will fight war at its most direct, at its most grotesque. If not exactly hand to hand then certainly eyeball to eyeball. So the death they know they face is turned into jokes — the blacker the better. I suppose it has always been the army way of coping. The move to the front has been made. Now they are marking time until the signal to battle. 'Advance to contact' is the phrase and then its not 'to battle' — the Jocks call it 'rock and roll'. "Let's get rocking and rolling," they say, meaning I guess, let's get up and at 'em.

I want to talk to Vincent Stott, not yet 17 and the youngest British soldier in the Gulf, to see if he was mellow. Back home in Edinburgh he couldn't even order a drink in his local pub, vote, or serve with the regiment in Northern Ireland. Yet here he is with a fixed bayonet and a baby face, a once a week shaver, waiting to play his part in the liberation of Kuwait. "How are you today Vince?" "Mellow." "How do you think you'll feel in battle?" "Mellow." At the moment you feel like saying yeah, great joke. now get back to Tynecastle school. But then the Royal Scots have a lot of these boy-men, another four 17 year olds. According to the Army the younger the soldier the better. An officer tells me that troops in their early twenties make the best infantry men. "They have a wild reckless-ness, an absolute belief they are going to survive. At 25 though, they start thinking about dying."

It is Norman Soutar's job to keep these boys finely balanced between 'mellow' and 'rocking and rolling'. A strong intelligent man, he looks older than his 30 years. In fact he has 12 years service in the regiment and will be leaving the army this summer, notwith-standing the local promotion which has made him the youngest major in the Gulf. He has welded A company into a fierce fighting force and is anxious to maintain battle readiness. The Scots Dragoon Guards had sent a messenger over the sands challenging his men to a game of volley ball. Norman sent him back with a flea in the ear. "Come back when we've finished what we're out here for," he said. So weapons cleaning is the number one priority. Sand drives into the SA 80 and 30 minutes each day are spent stripping down the work-ing parts and methodically cleaning them.

Zero Charlie, Captain Bruce's Warrior, is my new home. He and his section, two signallers, driver and gunner, nestle around it like chicks around a mother hen. She is quite simply, their life support system, and now she's mine. We eat off our knees inside, where a salt cellar hangs next to a copy of the 23rd Psalm, shelter inside her when it rains, and at night sleep outside beside her comforting tracks. The Warrior is the lynch pin of modern infantry combat. While the tanks may go first it is the infanteers who have inherited the glamour of the cavalry charge, spilling from the backs of their vehicles to take the enemy territory. Only a week ago, as we heard of the precision,

45

laser guided bombing of Iraq, it seemed inconceivable to think ultimately this war would end in the trenches. Unlike the tanks and planes whose targets are distant smudges, the infantry men are going to see their enemy.

Tonight we are invited to the Royal Scots orders meeting, known as the O group. Grey and ugly by day, at night the landscape is brilliant. I have never seen stars looking so bright and as we walk the two miles across the sands to regimental headquarters, Major Soutar points out the twinkling flashes of distant air-raids. Although both he and Major John Potter are against the idea, the commanding officer, Colonel Johnstone, wants the men to have some serious relaxation. Mobile showers, food which doesn't come out of a tin, and even some videos. "Like the First World War they can come out of their trenches for a while, but without the brothels I'm afraid, gentlemen," says the Colonel. Now O groups were officially strictly off-limit to us. Our information was to be carefully controlled but Johnstone has other ideas. As we stand afterwards sharing a sweet coffee, sipping from the same chipped mug, he tells us that if we are prepared to risk our necks with the Jocks, then we should know everything that they do. It seems a reasonable bargain and sitting in on the intelligence briefing we have learned more about where we are and what the mission is than at any other time. The British would be driving not into Kuwait, but straight into Iraq, where the enemy they face will almost certainly be Saddam's Republican Guards.

*Jan 29.* Awoken at 5.30 am. by American bombers streaming north. The hum of their engines was followed by the drum roll, thunder clap of carpet bombing. It is bitterly cold, and even though I had gone to bed fully dressed, I am freezing. The weather in the desert is capable of continuous tactical surprises. After the rains, the heaviest in a decade, have come bitter frosts, and water is frequently frozen first thing in the morning. Twice daily there is 'stand to', one of the oldest traditions of the army, as first light and dusk are the optimum times for enemy attack. At 6 am. and again at 6 pm. the Warriors are battened down for 30 minutes and we crowd inside sipping 'brews'. Unless the Colonel can fulfil his promise it looks like we will remain on compo food. There are six main meals in a ration box — steak and onion, steak and kidney (known as 'babies heads') stewed steak, steak goulash, corned beef and chicken in brown sauce. In addition there are tinned sausages and baconburgers for breakfast, and snacks like crackers with tins marked 'cheese, processed', known as 'cheese, possessed'. Each Warrior is packed with ration cartons and boxes of 'stickies', chocolate bars and biscuits the boys are sent from home.

Corporal David Knox is my guide for the day. An intense young man wearing puttees, he is a sniper, medic, signaller and barber, who specialises in Marine-style zero to three haircuts. A man of many talents but of few words. We attend a first aid class but it is too cold to concentrate. Up the road the Iraqis are undergoing a round the clock pounding from the air. It is so intense with 110,000 missions that the Allies nearly run out of bombs. At one time it was thought that destruction from the air could be completed in ten days, but resources had to be devoted to Scud hunting and poor weather has further hindered operations.

*Jan 30.* Under a full moon the "demoralised and defeated" Iraqi army invaded Saudi Arabia in three places, apparently in search of intelligence after being blinded by the air attacks. At Al Wafra 20 T55 tanks and 400 men caught the Allies by surprise and fought a fierce engagement. It was here that 11 American servicemen were accidentally killed by one of their own helicopters. But the main assault came at the border town of Khafji where a column of Iraqi tanks and armoured personnel carriers with up to 4000 troops broke across the border. The fighting lasted for 36 hours and the Iraqis fought with great courage and ferocity, before they were driven out, delivering a timely warning to allied commanders.

The British division is under Americans control, and there are problems to iron out. After eight hours bumping along in an open truck, rehearsals which involved passing through US lines, it is not difficult to work out the cunning plan. The Americans will breach the Iraqi fortifications, the great berms, tank traps and minefields, hold the position, and allow the British to pass through and engage the Iraqis behind.

We are joined by the Queen's Company of the Grenadier Guards. "Good," snorted one Scottish NCO, "we can fling them into the ditches and drive over them when we run out of facines." "If they don't get to fight the Iraqis then pretty soon they'll be fighting each other," an officer confided. Strategic sign posts marked 'Vermont', 'Wisconsin', 'Cherry' and 'Colorado' loom up out of the dark, alongside them gum-chewing US Military Policemen. They wave forlornly at the trucks of British troops — none is returned — MP in any language is a dirty word to private soldiers.

*Jan 31.* We join a church service for B company, although the chances of getting words and pictures past the army censors are remote indeed. There seems to be a terror of offending the Saudis which I mention to Major Potter. "If they want us here to defend their country then they are going to have to put up with our customs. We are not going to hide church away from you guys," he assured us.

I sent this despatch to the the Daily Mail with the approval of the censors.

The padre bounced across the desert in a Land Rover stripped down for warfare. He had taken a four pound hammer to the windscreen and all the other glass, and had etched the word 'chaplain' on the bonnet. Sporting a traditional shemagh head-dress, Stephen Blakey jumped into the sand with all the enthusiasm of a sergeant-major about to lead his men into battle. But the men who gathered at his feet had come looking for spiritual guidance to carry with them on the eve of conflict. He told them they had been sent by mankind to put right an evil-but that could not be achieved without cost. He was saying that while it would be nice if, for the task ahead, we prayed that God could put a shield around us -a sort of thickened body armour if you like — He did not deal in insurance policies.

The padre's delivery, in the plain, blunt language of the Royal Scots who faced him, boomed across the sand. This was a man of God who could see good in the right to wage war. Now, when I looked into the young faces rubbed raw by the wind and sun, I swear I could see a kind of contentment settle over them as they prayed. We were sitting cross-legged on the ground or on bunched-up packs of webbing, and we clasped the blue order-of-service books of the Church of Scotland. As a concession to the moment we discarded our helmets, but the weapons of war lay at our feet. There were 165 soldiers, B

Company's finest. Young men of extraordinary contradictions, with their cropped heads, tattooed biceps and dark glasses, their language coarse and studded with profanities but their boots polished to a parade ground shine for their appointment with the padre.

From the moment the opening bars of Highland Cathedral floated across our heads there was a growing anticipation. This was probably the last time Bravo Company would assemble for church before they were committed to battle. The padre had put up a trestle table, covering it with tartan and crisp white linen. From a travelling kit of sacraments he brought out a simple wooden cross and silver Communion cup. For bread he broke pieces of brown biscuit from a compo ration box. Unaccompanied by music, the men sang Fight the Good Fight, a hymn that could have been written for physical as much as spiritual conflict. And when the padre spoke, the soldiers turned their gaze up towards him. He was saying that this could be our last chance to reach an understanding with God.

In times of war men who would not step inside a church need to find an inner strength and comfort. And that is what is happening among the Royal Scots. Of all the British forces committed here, they are facing the greatest dangers. Trench warriors, they will be doing the hand-to-hand fighting. Their targets will be seen not from a cockpit or tank turret, but face-to-face at the end of their SA80s. Now we are being told we could not choose when we died. 'We need God for peace and courage in the days ahead, but He is not an insurance policy,' the chaplain said. 'It will require all of our inner strength, more than we have ever had. People will die and have died on our side not because they lived a good or bad life, but because mankind has got us into a war, because an evil has been done. We have to put that evil right, and the price of it is the lives of soldiers. In knowing what will happen, in knowing how many of us will die, we must get ourselves right with God. This may be our last opportunity, and we must do it as we prepare for war, because He will look after our souls and give us help to make us even better soldiers than we have trained to be. 'So we can go into our task in glory,honour and inner strength. For God inspires a deeper courage,a deeper strength.'

When it was over, the queue for men wanting Communion too was as long as that stretching from the padre's truck awaiting sweets and cigarettes. It had been a moment to savour, and afterwards we stood around in knots, all reluctant to move. They say here that courage is like a bank balance. Today all of us, soldiers and non-combatants alike, received a boost to our reserves we will surely need in the days ahead.

*Feb 1.* We return to the BAA and when our minders overhear myself, Robert Fox and others discussing our past few days in context with the allied offensive, they are horrified. We are accused of 'knowing the plan'. Gouldstone storms off to tell the Brigadier and returns in an even fouler mood. He is, really, being quite absurd. A complaint is made to the two senior Colonels at the FTU who insist we are driven down so they can give us a dressing-down. We are permitted to make phone calls but only in the presence of Captain Irvine. After all the silliness, the phone calls to home and office are a tremendous lift — a lifeline to sanity, and a reminder that we are after all, civilians. There is also mail to pick up — the first from home. That afternoon Hammerbeck comes across to see all the hacks, and in a calm, even voice, tells us why secrecy is so important. In equally calm, even voices, we tell him we know. "The Iraqis don't know we're here — they think we are still in the old location," he says. I am surprised they have even had time to wonder. With all those tons of ordnance that are falling on them, day in day out, I should think they have got more pressing needs. That evening Mike and I insist on being driven over to the Royal Scots, worried that we may have compromised our position with them. They are, of course, mellow.

Forty miles away on the Iraqi front lines, yellow lights are being projected on to the night sky like a movie projector. How much more can they take?

*Feb 2.* Christopher Hammerbeck was planning to prepare his men for battle. Emotional equipment he believed they needed every bit as much as physical training. It was to be an instructive weekend as I travelled with him by helicopter and Range Rover. The men of A Company of the Royal Regiment of Fusiliers snapped to attention as the Brigadier walked up. He opened with a friendly: "I am the chap who will send you into battle to do some crazy things." But courage and conviction was the order of the day.

"Sadly, you won't all come back, and I want you to understand that all of us are going to see some pretty terrible sights. Some pretty terrible sounds too. People burning to death and men screaming with their legs off." He went on: "It could trouble your sleep till your dying day. I know I shall be frightened. I know I shall have a dryness at the back of my throat." As he talked about the responsibility on everyone to have something to believe in, it seemed that this must have been the kind of fighting talk delivered by leaders to their men in past conflicts. If not for inspiration, then Hammerbeck knew the men looked to him for comfort, so he volunteered what he believed in. His Roman Catholic faith, his wife and his children. "I don't give a stuff what you believe in — it can be your home, your football club or your local pub. For me it is my family and God." Courage, he said, would come from exchanging worries, clearing the mental decks for action. Then we could take on the Iraqis — and stuff them.

Hammerbeck has read the Koran and understands, I think, the Arab mind, so it seems a good time to ask him why we are here and why young servicemen should be asked to lay down their lives for a country few had even heard of six months ago. "Sometimes I ask myself that, but then I think there is a principle at stake. The principle that says big, aggressive countries should not be allowed to get away with invading their smaller neighbours." But supposing Kuwait only grew oranges I thought to myself. After all, there has been no worldwide coalition to 'rescue' Lebanon, frequently invaded by more powerful neighbours.

The Brigadier has a poem pinned to a notice board in the Land Rover that serves as his private quarters. It was written by a French monk and sent to Hammerbeck by Chris Keeble, the Falklands soldier who took over 3 Para, when Colonel H. Jones was killed. It read:

*"I abandon myself to You. Do with me as You will. Whatever You may do with me, I thank You. I am prepared for anything. I accept everything. Provided Your will is fulfilled in me and in all creatures, I ask for nothing more, my Lord."*

Life out here encourages us to be loners, and Hammerbeck who writes a daily letter to his wife, Alison, as well as keeping a very detailed journal, is no exception. He is reading Byron from whose turbulent mind he, apparently, draws relaxation.

*Feb 3.* Our minder is complaining about our behaviour. Since I am determined that he shall not be allowed to jeopardise things for us I say nothing about it. But it provokes an argument between Mike and me. He accuses me of supinely accepting all the rules and regulations. We must remember we are civilians, he says. More mail from England, including a strip cartoon that shows two tired old hacks, watching Scud wars, sitting in the comfort of their hotel bedrooms. "Of course," says one, "the war will shift to the infantry soon and we will revert to more traditional journalistic practice." The other replies "Sitting in our hotel rooms and making it all up?" "Exactly."

The weather continues unpredictable. Now we are enduring a dust storm. It is the season of 'shamal', the north west winds which drive a curtain of sand that would strip the paint off cars. Groping through the winds to the cookhouse you are forced to use your entire body as a windbreak while gobbling down your food to cut out the contamination of the desert.

*Feb 4.* Back with the battle group and another long exercise called an FTX. For 36 hours we trundle round the desert following coordinates that are supposed to prepare us for battle. Forming up as a battalion, passing through an imaginary breach, and attacking an imaginary enemy. Only I don't think much of it goes to plan, it seems the American MPs set off so fast they left us behind. We move in convoy at such slow speeds it relieves any element of dash. But it does give us time to ponder on mine fields. Mine fields, we know, are one of Iraq's main defences and the Warrior although up-armoured and able to withstand rocket propelled grenades when it comes to mines is very vulnerable. There is no reinforcement on the floor but commanders enquiries about obtaining sandbags have got nowhere. It reminds me of all those sandbags I had seen back in Dhahran before Christmas when sappers were building a piece of art for the amusement of the Prince of Wales. But if there are no sandbags there are at least bungees. Forget about discipline and training — these elasticated straps were what keep the army on the move in the desert. On the outside of vehicles sleeping bags, rucksack and kit are all lashed down by the bungee, while inside they are a kind of safety rail preventing saucepans and supplies from hitting you on the head. "Never mind their guns — the only thing to upset the boys is losing a bungee — they are like a close friend and are in very short supply," Norman Soutar says.

*Feb 5.* Long night time exercises are a time to talk and there is a natural curiosity about the role of the Special Air Service — universally referred to by their less elite comrades as the 'Hereford Hooligans'. I wonder if that means the special boat section were known as the 'Plymouth Brethren'. I know that a full SAS squadron had been detached to the Gulf back in August but as one of their former colleagues told me: "They were like caged lions and they were pulled back to Cyprus for a further two months to cool down." By the time the war started they had returned to the desert and were operating behind enemy lines. It is not easy to know what exactly their brief was, apart from disruption and chaos. Certainly, a prime objective was mobile Scud launchers. By using laser targetting they could guide allied bombers to them. A beam, invisible to the naked eye, laser targetting was one of the great successes of the air war. The SAS also were critical in destroying much of Saddam's command control on the ground. While it is unlikely that they carried out individual assassinations, I was told they were responsible for blowing up Iraqi O group meetings which had a shattering effect on enemy morale. They were successful too in rescuing allied pilots, both American and British who had been forced to ditch their aircraft after having been hit by anti-aircraft fire over Iraqi positions. Back in December I recalled that the SAS had been credited with stealing a Scud and spiriting it back across the desert to Dhahran. This had always seemed far fetched. The Scuds were a crude, fuel-driven missile, based on the same technology that propelled Hitler's V2s across the Channel, 45 years earlier. According to my ex-SAS friend, the 'Hereford Hooligans' had actually been bringing back defecting members of Saddam's air command. Perhaps another reason why the skies have been so empty of Iraqi fighters. But the SAS's principal role was to locate and destroy chemical stock piles and the factories that produced them. We did not know it yet, but the destruction was so exact it must have saved 10,000 lives. They had also supplied new information about Iraqi attempts at confusing the allies damage assessment. The deception involved burning oil soaked rags on top of their tanks and APCs to give an impression of a "kill".

*Feb 6.* The 'Forces Echo' the army's own newspaper had become required reading, though not for its news coverage. 4th Brigade was still waiting for the first reports that it was actually in the desert! No, what made the bulletins so indispensable were the lonely hearts columns, full of schoolboy double entendres and spicier invitations. Officers and men took to them with relish, peppering their replies with the same quasi-suggestive phrases. Through the BFPO 3000 scheme soldiers were still receiving fat postbags. Brigadier Hammerbeck was writing to five schools, while others had inadvertently found their mail increasing after appearing in the press. After I had reported some of his more bloodthirsty remarks, Colonel Johnstone for example, had received a letter from an indignant Scottish preacher appalled by his blunt language. But perhaps the biggest victim of all was Private Stott. After his exposure as the Gulf's youngest soldier, poor Vincent had been overwhelmed with letters — not just those inquiring after his health. There were proposals of love and marriage and proposals of a different kind, from men drawn to his boyish good looks. After he had received 70 he appealed to me: "Please tell the people of Britain don't send me any more letters," but still they kept coming.

*Feb 7.* The 'Hack Pack' is back together, and rather miserable. After all this time there are uncertainties about whether the army will be able to get our film and copy out once the ground war starts. We all wonder what we are doing here. None of our minders seem to understand the perishable nature of news. But never mind, there are 14 letters waiting for me and a parcel of oranges, apples, loo paper, newspapers and money. Nearly 1000 dollars. Both Mike and I have been thinking of what we should do should hostilities cease. The story will still be to get to Kuwait City so we decide to keep one change of civilian clothing with us and as much money as we can.

They are putting on videos in the cookhouse, and appropriately today's is 'Lawrence of Arabia' which someone scornfully remarks is more akin to 'Carry on Camping'. I am determined to catch up on letter writing. Something Hammerbeck said to me keeps coming back. His greatest fear was not what he called "the living or dying thing" but not measuring up — not being able to do what he is paid to do. I don't suppose I am frightened for myself — that will probably come afterwards — but for everyone at home. Somehow they all seem much more vulnerable than me.

*Feb 8.* The NAAFI has finally arrived in the desert, selling stickies, disposable razors, and even aftershave. The soldiers there have adopted a litter of puppies, found abandoned in the streets of Jubail. Imaginatively they have called them Scud, Saddam, Des and Snifftest. There's a breeze in the air and, never one to scorn a good drying day I spend half an hour rinsing out some underpants in the miserably small amount of water we are allowed. The water bowser hasn't arrived so I have to scrounge some extra from the cookhouse. David Irvine — we are all trying to get along now — tells of an extraordinary trip he made to Australia when he was 19. Apparently he went to work for the Duchess of York's sister, Jane, and her husband, Alex. This was in 1983, three years before the Royal wedding, but Jane insisted then that her little sister would marry Prince Andrew. Anyway, Alex had a prize goat that would lunge at anyone who passed by, and one night after too much bourbon, Irvine shot the bugger dead. I think his working holiday ended soon after.

*Feb 9.* US Defence Secretary, Richard Cheney, and Gen. Colin Powell, Chairman of the Joint Chiefs of Staff, visited Saudi Arabia to be briefed by the Generals and decide on a date for the ground offensive. Schwarzkopf favoured more time for the air assault and for preparing for the land war, but diplomatic and political pressure was mounting. 4th Brigade were holding a field day for COs, company commanders and logistic and brigade staff. Hammerbeck wanted to caution his senior men that although action was approaching it was at least a week, to a week-and-a-half away. Impress on the men, he said, that the longer the air war went on, the better it would be for them: "We must develop a sense of comradeship and corporate identity. It is that which is going to mark us out in the time ahead, and in 20 years time inspire us to want to meet again at the Cavalry Club."

During tea break a couple of officers confided to me they were worried about the Brigadier. "All this leading from the front stuff, he could be the H. Jones of this campaign," said one. Colonel Jones had been killed leading a courageous advance on Argentine positions at Goose Green. He and Sergeant Ian McKay were both posthumously awarded the Victoria Cross. I learned that should anything happen to Hammerbeck he will be replaced by either Iain Johnstone of the Royal Scots, or David Radcliffe of the Royal Artillery. An officer who served in the Falklands said: "You know the Brigadier has been built up so much by you guys and the TV that if anything goes wrong with 4th Brigade he will become the public scapegoat." Well that seemed quite fair to me, he was the man in charge and he would reap the glory if all went well, and should carry the can if it didn't. I remembered that the Brigadier, like every private soldier here, reckoned that this would be the highlight of his career. "Next stop the lecture circuit. The Army have got more Brigadiers than they'll ever need under Options for Change," he had said.

The field day in fact, turned out to be an opportunity for some well disguised but heavy side-swipes between the armour and the infantry. Foot soldiers have long distrusted the 'tankies' and the feeling was reciprocated. Colonel Vickery, for the tanks, insisted that at close range to the enemy, say 200 metres, his Challengers could be vulnerable. It was the infantry's job to protect them. For the troops though, Colonel Johnstone warned: "the speed of the caravan is that of the slowest camel, and we have some very slow camels." That night Major Gouldstone turned a couple of tins of compo sausage into a very acceptable Ghurka curry — hot and spicy.

*Feb 10.* Mike Moore and I had been invited to Sunday lunch with A squadron of the Life Guards, and as usual our minder had left us with a hefty walk to find them. Maybe it was just the sun but as we tramped across the desert to their position the site shimmered in and out of our vision. It was like stumbling on a mirage — ahead sat a group of young, tanned men, at tables and chairs, but I suppose after several weeks of desert life behind us, where battle readiness had necessarily taken precedence over more civilised eating habits, the unusual easily assumed that of a vision. It immediately conjured up a picture of Battle of Britain fliers, dozing in the Kent sunshine in Lloyd Loom chairs. The only thing that seemed to be missing was a faithful black labrador. I suppose though you would expect the Life Guards to push the boat out. Like the Queen's Company of the Grenadier Guards, the Life Guards had been sent to the Gulf piecemeal. One squadron strong of 14 Challengers, they were the armoured wing of the Royal Scots battle-group. But they maintained a fierce identity. The squadron's ensign of claret and blue floated in the breeze as we sat down to a marvellous spaghetti bolognese, laced with garlic, washed down with cans of Moussy, alcohol free beer. James Hewitt, the squadron's laconic commanding officer, with a David Niven profile, held court. At 32, he had a local promotion as Major but had still to sit exams to ensure that he held on to the rank. A polo-playing friend of the Prince of Wales, he resigned from the Guards Polo Club after it drove out his friend Major Ronald Ferguson, the Prince's polo manager. Both men had the same two goal handicap. He had also helped Princess Diana master her fear of riding. An Anglo-Irish, he had named his tank 'Lifford', after the small County Donegal town where he was born. He has arranged the most stylish ending to the war too. Even before they have fired a shot in anger, a polo match, not in tanks but on horseback between the 4th and 7th Brigades. He did not know it then but it was to take more than 5 months to come to fruition.

The 103 men that he commanded had an average age of 23, and as they swarmed over three tanks to pose up for a photograph that would go in the regimental scrapbook, it seemed a tragedy that any of them should have to be injured or even die. The regiment of course has battle honours won from all corners of the old Empire. For some, like Lt. Piers German, there was a personal badge of courage to wear. A century ago, his great-great-uncle's heroism earned him the Victoria Cross at Rourke's Drift, the epic battle of the Zulu wars. Lt. Gonville (Piers's middle name) Bromhead, was of course played on film by Michael Caine. At 21, Piers had followed his god-father into the Life Guards and christened his Challenger Bromhead, and while he hoped the famous name would bring him luck, memory was proving both an inspiration and a responsibility.

No.1 troop were preparing for their weekly foot inspection when Mike and I sauntered over. After all the 'on the brink of battle' stories, we both realised this would make a splendid antidote. First we lined them up, trousers rolled to the knees, and their officer, the Racing Post reading, Lt. James Gaselee, got down on his knees to check their toes for foot rot. We guessed right. The Sun newspaper loved it and littering it with puns like "cultured conk" (James went to Charterhouse) and "the desert rots" gave it prominence under the headline "Best foot forward lads, here we toe."

The Challengers were rightly praised for their role in the Gulf but before the crisis there had been doubts over their future with the Army. Their performance in desert conditions though, is in marked contrast to their capability on home turf in Europe. There they had been plagued by breakdowns. Like a rarely used, much prized car, lying idle brought on faults, but in the desert the tank was being used every day. At 62 tons and with a gun capable of hitting its target at 2000 metres the army had added a formidable third force to make it a real battle winner. Up-armouring, a coat of reactive armour which, thanks to a chemical reaction can absorb and smother shell fire, was another of Britain's secret weapons in the war. It was also remarkably easy to assemble, as I discovered that evening helping Lt. Philip Earl and 3 Troop put the finishing touches to their tanks. It seemed remarkably simple. Like chunky squares of chocolate, you just bolt it on.

*Feb 11.* From the Life Guards we decided to move across to the three neighbouring squadrons of the 14th/20th King's Hussars. They seemed to specialise in out of the way war honours. Baghdad and Mesopotamia in 1917, more recently Medicinia in Northern Italy in 1945. Then the regiment was commanded by Col. H.A. Tilney, whose son, Major Godfrey Tilney, is second in command in the desert. Sons, grandsons, and great-grandsons abound in the regiment still. The other day the new, adjutant Captain Andrew Gossage discovered a letter from his great grandfather, a squadron leader in the Great War. "Dear George," it ran "the horse was shot from under me the other day and lost all my kit. Please send a new coffee pot."

As we arrived at B Squadron so too did Brigadier Hammerbeck, who had come to give the same pep talk we had heard a week ago delivered to the infantry. So for a while I dozed in the sun. Suddenly we were whisked with almost indecent haste, to a firing range, and invited to have a go with Browning 9 mm pistols, Sterling sub-machine guns, and that old army favourite, the Bren gun. There was no limit on ammunition and we didn't need to be asked twice. Thank God all those sanctimonious critics who had taken such pleasure in writing off the various abilities of the MRT reporters, couldn't see us. In letters from colleagues I learned there had been the inevitable envious attacks on our credentials, a royal correspondent indeed!, and the fact that we had compromised our independence by putting on uniform and becoming quasi-soldiers. What tosh! What did they suggest we wore — dinner jackets? I didn't want to be shot, but I certainly didn't want to be shot by my own side. Nor do I apologise for writing 'my side.' The idea of meeting out overtly even handed reporting is naive in the extreme — we were part of the war effort. Presumably the Iraqis had their MRTs too. We must have spent an hour spraying bullets, with indifferent results, into a sand bank. It was not until a few days later we discovered why we had been moved so quickly. Within minutes of Hammerbeck completing his tonic to the troops one of them quietly went out of sight, climbed into a tank, and shot himself in the leg. It wasn't life threatening but it meant he would take no further part in the war.

That night at an O group, back with the Royal Scots, Colonel Johnstone tells his men that the air war has continued to devastate the Iraqi forces his men face across the sands. The Tawakana division of the Republican Guard in particular, have been reduced by 45% effectiveness. Of 222 tanks, 151 were destroyed, while of 90 artillery pieces, 22 had been put out of action.

*Feb 12.* For the first time the desert echoed to the sounds of the parade ground. All 880 men of the Royal Regiment of Fusiliers have formed up for a unique group photograph. Dust churned off the desert as sergeant majors wheeled their companies into ruler-straight columns. Tanks, Warriors, Sultan and Scimitar reconnaissance vehicles, trucks and Land Rovers were called in for the historic occasion. In all 160 track and wheeled vehicles. The commanding officer, Lt. Col. Andrew Larpent cannot contain his pride as the sight unfolds. Larpent, just 40, is the youngest CO in the division. There is a bitter wind, and we wait hunkered against a Land Rover, as a helicopter circles constantly allowing Mike Moore and ITN to take pictures from the air. Though the pictures that everyone remembers were not of man and machines stock still at attention but opportunities Mike at least spotted as we waited for the battle group to arrive. One was from a tank as a squadron moved, spread across the desert, and the other of men wheeling into line to the shout of a sergeant major. Major Alistair Wicks offered us a lift back to his squadron headquarters and we asked our minder to collect us later. It turned out to be a terrible mistake. I needed to make a phone call home after a particularly worrying letter and I had intended to ask Irvine to drive me to the FTU, although my heart sank at the prospect of spending hours watching his painful navigation, getting us progressively more lost. By chance, as we waited for Irvine to collect us, Dave Lee, a Quarter-Master Sergeant who had been running the shooting range the previous day, drove past and offered us a lift to the nearest town, Hafra Al Batin. "But isn't it out of bounds?" I enquired. "Certainly not," he said, "we can go in and out as we like." He had a letter for us too, from colleagues. To me it seemed too good an opportunity to miss. But when Mike doubted the wisdom of such a trip I pointed out that only that morning both an intelligence major at the BAA and a Captain in the Military Police had both told me independently that Hafra was not closed. This was curious because Gouldstone had reneged on a promise to take the MRT there for a day out. We all wanted to get some laundry done and have some decent food. But he had abruptly announced that the town was out of bounds to everyone. So as we bumped across the desert in the back of a Land Rover, I reassured Mike that all would be well. It was a 40 minute trip and every couple

Trench trap: Captain Irvine finds himself in a familiar position

of miles or so Lee stopped the engine and jumped out to place luminous yellow cylumes in the sand, markers for our return home.

We knew Hafra would be crawling with reporters, the Army-
christened 'unilaterals' and we were both most anxious to avoid the
'hack-pack'. At an hotel where we knew we could telephone, Lee
went in first to check the coast was clear, returning to my astonish-
ment with my friend and colleague, David Williams, who was dressed
in army uniform. "We've all got it — how do you think we get past the
check points? They've tried to run reporters out of this town," he
said. So that's why it took so long to get our second pair of DPs. They
were all being flogged on the black market back in Dhahran. However, our immediate fear was that someone would report our presence, even though we had been assured that the town was not off-
limits. Certainly the place was crawling with military — Americans,
Saudis, French, and stacks of British. Anyway we were hustled into
an upstairs room at the hotel. It was a brief but emotional visit, and
two hours later after phone calls, and being fed on pizzas and watered
(someone had even got hold of some illicit Scotch) we prised Sergeant
Lee away from an interview with a Middle East journalist and headed
back to the desert. We learned one thing: those colleagues of ours
knew more about the proposed attack than we did and they also knew
it was imminent.

Despite everything our unease was confirmed as we reached the
sentry point for the Hussars, and Lee leaped out to book in. There
was a massive search out for us. Within a few minutes one of our
minders was on the scene to tell it all himself, and didn't Captain
David Scoular relish it. In short we had apparently jeopardized the
equivalent of the Normandy landings. What rubbish! But Scoular
was only warming up. We would be slung out of the desert at first
light. We had ruined a good soldiers career. It went on and on. Somehow I didn't think the blunt Lancastrian, Dave Lee, was going to
suffer. There followed a confrontation with Mike Gouldstone. There
were no white lights of interrogation— just the instruction to have
everything packed. It was not a good night.

*Feb 13.* We are hanging on to our position in the MRT by our fin-
gertips. The story of our indiscretion has gone onwards and upwards,
we are told, to the very ears of General Rupert Smith, the commander
of the British division. After what we have learned in Hafra the Gen-

eral may just have more important things on his mind, never mind what the Iraqis have in store for us. Like miscreant schoolboys we are metaphorically made to wait outside the headmaster's study. Eventually the joy comes back — in our favour. It was our Waterloo. I was grateful to Col. Vickery too for the way he handled the matter.

Later we are taken to view a remarkable logistics operation. In the middle of the desert a camp full of bunk beds, showers and a cookhouse. This oasis of comfort is not for British soldiers but their Iraqi prisoners. Commanders estimate they will process 2,000 POWs and deserters each day, but so impressive are the facilities that as they await their first inmates, the guards from the King's Own Scottish Borderers, and the Royal Highland Fusiliers are living themselves in the prisoners compound. It would, I thought, be the envy of the men at the front on rationed water and beds of sand, and it almost certainly promised infinitely better conditions for the poor Iraqis across the desert. Colditz it certainly isn't, in fact it had the feel of an hotel and the style of a holiday camp. Helpful signs in Arabic point the way for arriving prisoners, directing them down five lanes marked with white tape, to a processing centre where Army clerks sit at lap-top computers, for all the world like hotel receptionists. Name, rank, serial number and date of birth are entered in line with the Geneva convention. For those brave enough to volunteer them, family addresses are also stored. Addresses are also passed on to the Red Cross who are able to contact loved ones. Here Officers and men will be segregated and each guest — sorry, prisoner — will receive a plastic identification tag. A medical check up follows before each man receives £150 worth of kit, two blankets, a poncho, mess tins and spoons, and a chemical suit to protect him from his own army's noxious gasses. So many prisoners are expected the camp has a stockpile of 19,600 respirators. Nothing has been overlooked. The army cooks have even ordered 500,000 ready-to-eat Muslim vegetarian meals. The camp commander, Major Andrew Robotham, a Coldstream guardsman, later to leave the army to pursue a career in politics, (inheriting Nigel Lawson's Leicestershire constituency) makes no apologies for the luxuries he has prepared: "We will be feeding them better food than they have had in their own front lines. Three hot meals a day, plus facilities for them to cook their own food too." There is barely time to wonder if Saddam has installed similar well appointed reception areas for coalition POWs before we are introduced to more enticing facilities — individual shower cubicles with enough fresh water for ritual washing and even a personal copy of the Koran. There are, of course, barbed wire and searchlights too, but they are more likely to be scanning the perimeter for Iraqis trying to break in.

Back at the BAA soldiers are still sending the last of their Valentines cards. The cards are ghastly creations that appeared to have fallen off the back of an East German lorry. We all mark our envelopes: "Warning — Army issue Valentine card".

*Feb 14.* Washing had become a peculiar skill. Each man with the Royal Scots was limited to 4 litres of water a day, for drinking, to wash in and for rinsing clothes. It was a meagre allowance and it added a new dimension to the regimental motto — 'Touch me with impunity.' But it was a daily challenge that the soldiers of B company rose to with a relish. Stripping down in the desert, even for us non-combatants, no longer seemed the height of immodesty. Each morning the red plastic bowl the six of us in Major Potter's section shared was religiously passed from man to man for the washing detail. Three inches of ice cold water poured with precision into the bowl were sufficient for shaving and to sponge oneself down. Instead of throwing it away, the brackish water was then used to steep clothes, which we threaded through the camouflage netting to dry. It was scarcely hygienic but it gave you an enormous sense of well being afterwards. Hygiene however, was critical. Army issue unscented talcum powder was liberally applied, but like any war campaign, many of the soldiers found themselves with foot problems. Parcels for me from home that day included one from an old soldier who had thoughtfully included a tin of foot powder.

At last orders have come through for the British forces to make their final move to the front — code named 'Forward Area Ray'. We are to move as a division, practising passing one Brigade through the other, and in battle groups completing a set of objectives. The exercise will take 48 hours and will be the biggest undertaking by a British military force since the Second World War. Our route will curiously be south west before turning north, and 4th Brigade must attack objectives Gold, Bronze and Silver. In all the move is only about 60 miles but according to Brigadier Hammerbeck it is designed to retain our 'opaqueness'. Saddam knows he is going to be attacked but he doesn't know where, when or by whom. There is a

Home made shower leaves no room for modesty

feeling that at last we are about to start 'rocking and rolling'. Mike and I ruthlessly pare down our kit even more, burning unwanted clothes and letters. All around us trenches are being filled in and acrid smoke drifts across the camp as gash pits are burned off. In a while there will be little trace of our presence. At dusk as we clamber into NBC suits a few rounds of artillery tracer arced lazily into the sunset, and in the sky a squadron of A 10s, one of the great success stories of the air war, pass on a hunting mission. The US air force had seen no future for the planes, whose ugliness was matched by the nick-name — 'wart hog' but the army had other ideas. Their success in destroying Iraqi armour, particularly tanks, was unsurpassed.

Colonel Johnstone meanwhile, has sent orders to the drivers of Land Rovers and trucks in the battle groups support echelons. All soft skinned vehicles must remove their windscreens. Johnstone, 42, is not a man to be trifled with. An expert on desert warfare he was decorated for his part in the Dhofar war, and he knows that glass can send a reflection 20 kilometres across this flat , monochrome landscape. It is for our protection. The goggles we all wear against the driving sand are bad enough. Iraqi helicopter gunships are certain to seek out the easier unprotected targets, such as Land Rovers. However, to the Colonel's consternation no other battle group issues a similar order and it remains a directive unique to the Royal Scots.

A former defence attache at the British Embassy in Beirut, Johnstone was on duty there the day Terry Waite, the Archbishop of Canterbury's envoy, was kidnapped in 1987. A few days after the kidnapping he was at a diplomatic cocktail party when a prominent militia man walked up to him and said: "Tell me Colonel, what does it feel like to be the No. 1 kidnap target in Beirut?" Johnstone's reply was blunt and the following day he recruited a militia of his own, 100-strong to guard the Embassy and its employees. A fluent Arab speaker, he of all the senior officers in the brigade, remains convinced that a ground war is inevitable. We leave at dusk, another great desert caravan, routing past a Bedouin village. It is a far cry from the romantic Hollywood image of great white tents just a jumbled collection of broken down huts. Sure there are a few mangy camels, but they are tethered to big shiny Chevrolet pick-up trucks. In the stop-start fashion of mechanised manoeuvre we lurch on our path throughout the night. Inside the Warrior, despite the discomfort, it is difficult to stay awake because of the heat.

*Feb 15.* At 7.30 am. the orders are to halt. Eager to see our new front line position we stumble bleary-eyed out of the vehicle, and, much to our surprise the landscape is physically different. True it is still desert, but we are on a broad plain, rising steeply to a ridge across to the left. The perspective provides perfect viewing for the American helicopters which sweep up behind us like the salute at Trooping the Colour before dropping over the horizon. We wait in the desert. 'Watty', Private Les Watt, stretches out in the driver's seat and sleeps soundly. Designed by an orthopaedic surgeon, the reclining seat is probably the Warrior's one and only luxury. Seven hours later at 2.30 pm Potter returned breathless from an O group, and dug out his tiny radio. "Something's up", he says. Twelve minutes later the something manifested itself on 'Desert Shield', the US forces network. Iraq is ready to call it a day. For a moment we all allow our hopes to gallop as Saddam's promise to pull out of Kuwait crackles tinnily over a thousand transistors. While no one is actually cheering there are all around fleeting looks of hope. The American newscaster sums it up: "If this is true there are going to be a lot of happy campers," he intones. But even as we listen we know there is one word missing from Iraq's terms — unconditional. Saddam must have been aware that the final act was about to begin; a ground offensive of such power and precision that would never be matched. Potter gathered his own junior O group, the 3 platoon commanders, artillery and Milan mortar section, REME crew, and company sergeant major. As they stood, their feet unconsciously drew diagrams in the sand while the Major reminded them that Saddam had tried similar stunts before. Don't forget last Christmas, he said, when the Allies began to dramatically increase their strength the dictator abruptly decided to free the western hostages. "Treat this with extreme caution — he is not saying 'I surrender, I will withdraw'. Don't let the men get optimistic because demands are bound to follow." A straw poll of the company revealed that more of my old prejudices about soldiers needed to be radically modernised. After all the talk only a couple of weeks ago about kills, the troops virtually to a man could not conceal their delight at the prospect of going home without a fight. What did cross their minds though, was the very real prospect that they may remain in the desert a lot longer to supervise a peace rather than wage a short sharp war.

Two hours later and Potter's words were looking prophetic. Now the radio talked of a string of preconditions attached to an Iraqi withdrawal. Of all people, Saddam was making demands. It began to provoke thoughts of allied garrisons in the desert, which by summer would see the great alliance of nations start to melt away. It also provoked some wry alternative conditions. Yes, Saddam would withdraw as long as the allies provided him with a year's supply of Big Macs, a subscription to 'Sky' (the only one in Iraq) and 637 virgins. What was more puzzling was not whether Saddam withdraws his forces from Kuwait but could he if he wanted to? In Riyadh Stormin Norman promised 'free passage' for Iraqi troops, provided they started to retreat in sufficient numbers. But so successful had the American strategic bombing been, that scarcely a single bridge between southern Iraq and Kuwait was still standing. For the Allies too there was the need to caution pleasure at the ground war being averted with the avowed aim of their major mission — the total and utter destruction of Saddam's army preventing him from starting another conflict in the region for years to come. By nightfall the remainder of the exercise had been cancelled and we have moved to our new position.

*Feb 16.* By early morning the talk of peace had evaporated even more, underlined by the vapour trails of F15 Eagles, and the steady drone of the B52s, making no attempt to conceal their presence, so convinced are they that they rule the skies. Information is a precious commodity. As with most supplies from the quartermaster's stores, there is either too much or too little. Sages here like to quote General Patton's remarks such as "more life may trickle out of man through thoughts than through a gaping wound." For the commanders information is almost on tap: satellite pictures, photos from Tornado reconnaissance planes, from the questioning of prisoners, and from cameras attached to missiles. But for the rest of us it is the radio. Either the BBC's World Service, or the racier 'Desert Shield', the American's "wizard" 106 FM transmission. It is a steady diet of fact, fiction, comment and some blatant propaganda. The despatches from the BBC are naturally of a higher quality, especially those of Mark Laity, their defence correspondent. With the broadcasts though, comes a deluge of new jargon. In its way a cosy caricature of war. Thus we have 'collateral damage'. In plain terms it means the bombs or guns hit something they did not intend, bluntly a 'miss'. Civilians are the victims of collateral damage. The toll of destruction is called 'writing down' or 'degradation'. Troops, bridges, tanks and ammunition dumps are no longer killed or even blown up but 'written down'. Trickiest among these brutal abstractions is 'battle damage assessment' or BDA. Another scarce commodity, this should tell us what damage the air raids have actually done rather than what the pilots think they have done. Aerial bombardment is never launched, ordered or executed, but in the sepulchral voices of the allied spokesman in Riyadh, faithfully broadcast each day, they are 'choreographed'. It certainly put into context the sight of three homeward bound B52s, which shimmered through the sky, leaving trails of spun pink sugar. On the ground the British commanders have taken to this new language with gusto, larding it with abstract tactical concepts in German. The war will be fought with 'fingerpitzgefuhle' or 'finger tip control' where the commander can probe at the enemy with his tanks. But the most popular word of this tactic-speak is 'Auftragstaktik' or mission oriented orders. The idea is that every man should know enough of the over-all plan to be able to use his initiative in his part of the enterprise. Therefore, each level of command is given the plan that has been revealed two levels above. Christopher Hammerbeck is saying he knows what the American corps commander has been ordered. Colonel Johnstone of the Royal Scots knows General Smith,the British Divisional commander's intelligence, and the process goes down through company and squadron commanders to platoon and troop leaders. Smith, Hammerbeck and Johnstone are all enthusi-asts of the doctrine. Rupert Smith has spent several hours discussing plans and concepts with groups of young officers and NCOs, win-ning considerable respect and admiration in the process. Smith's desire to communicate at all levels of his command must, I think, be due to his training as a paratrooper. Paras drop in tight units of four and may be dispersed all over the place if things go wrong, hence the watchword of the Parachute Regiment is "every soldier must know his task and mission." Among the men of the 4th Brigade, it has to be said, there is little evidence that the new doctrine is turning the troopers into Prussian guards. Their tactical principles are those of British soldiers through the years — muddle through and see what you can get off the CQMS when nobody's looking.

Among the Royal Scots however, there are two favourite adjec-tives — 'outstanding' and 'outrageous'. The Jocks, the private sol-diers, are according to their officers, simply outstanding.The hair-cuts, shorn to the scalp, of which perhaps Major Potter's is the most extreme, are 'outrageous'. The regiment is of course, imbued with history. War is their business and has been so for centuries. The oldest and most senior regiment in the Army, it received its Royal Charter in 1633 but had been around in one form or another long before. In fact, it is reckoned to be the oldest regiment to have seen continuous service in the world, a claim challenged only by a couple of long-defunct Spanish units and the Picardy regiment of France. It was a Picard who, according to legend, once boasted: "We guarded the tomb of Christ," to which a Royal Scot replied "If we'd been Pontius Pilate's bodyguard, He would never have got away." The nickname Pontius Pilate's bodyguards, stuck. John Potter believes his men are the best the British army has to offer. "They are like weasels, great fighters when they go into the trenches only medics,

Waiting

mullahs and those surrendering with their hands in the air will be spared," he says.

If the Falklands was essentially a West Country affair, much of the Navy and Royal Marines strength is raised west of the Avon, then the Gulf conflict is shaped by the accents of Lancashire, Ulster, Northumbria, the Midlands, and particularly Scotland. Scottish soldiers crop up everywhere. Quite apart from the men on attachment, like the section of Queen's Own Highlands serving with the Fusiliers, Scotsman feature among the support battalions of engineers and signals. Wholly Scottish regiments, like the Royal Scots, recruit exclusively in Edinburgh, Lothian and the Lowlands, which makes Private Christopher Owen rare indeed. But among the men of A company he enjoys a peculiar status. Not only is he English, he is the only direct descendant of a Victoria Cross holder on Gulf duty. On October 15th 1918 in the dying days of the First World War, his grandfather R.E. Elcock, then a 19 year old corporal, rushed his Lewis gun team to within 10 yards of German guns which had been causing mayhem among British troops. His extraordinary heroism put the enemy machine gun out of action, led to the capture of 5 prisoners, and allowed the allied advance on the western front to continue. Later that same day he repeated the bravery, and was awarded the highest medal for valour. The medals which are part of the Royal Scots illustrious history, remain in Edinburgh Castle, but a glimpse of the citation at 13, motivated a grandson he never knew to follow him into the infantry. Corporal Elcock had enlisted in the Royal Scots simply because the battalion happened to be garrisoned in his home town of Wolverhampton at the time. For Christopher Owen, with a thick Black Country accent, there was only one regiment to join, even if it meant a 300 mile trip from his home town, Stoke on Trent to Edinburgh. It has brought him an inevitable nickname 'the Pommie', and a sense of history — "I know I mustn't let the family down," he says.

In the hour before dusk men are sitting cross-legged in the sand, sorting and sifting kit. They have adapted jet packs on their chest webbing, and each bulges with ammunition and grenades. Bandoliers of tracer loop across their bodies. Some stuff bullets into pouches on their helmets. Others are scientifically covering every piece of metal, however dull, on their SA80s with camouflage tape, to reduce further the risk of glare. Only bayonets do not receive this treatment, the sun striking the tips in a splash of bloody red. Personal kit has been reduced to a minimum too — one rucksack for 5 men. It is easy to think, looking at these weatherbeaten young faces that there will be disappointment if their test does not come. But that would be an insult to their professionalism. They have made the mental adjustment necessary to go to war. A sort of understanding if you like. But if their orders take them away from the front, there will be no complaints.

*Feb 17*. At first we had to cup hands to ears to hear the high explosive bursting over the Iraqi positions. The wind had sent a curtain of sand tearing across the desert and for hours the men squatted inside Warriors out of the blinding storm. Now nothing surely, would prevent a land offensive for the guns firing up ahead of us were British. A drum roll of explosions shook the ground, and we flipped off radios to venture out into the dust storm. There were something like 350 Howitzers firing 155 mm shells from 12 miles onto Iraqi positions in an operation called 'shoot and scoot'. The big guns were trundled into position and each loosed off 40 rounds of the huge 106 lbs shells before swiftly packing up, moving on, and starting again. The idea was to fire and move before the Iraqi artillery could get a trace on the British position. It was a double-edged plan. Any Iraqi gun emplacements tempted to return fire would then be flattened by batteries of multi-launch rockets which send their missiles even further — up to 20 miles. The rockets were fired in salvos of 12 and delivered nearly 8000 separate bomblets. They were what the Jocks would call an 'outstanding piece of kit', each capable of devastating an area 500 yards square. The thuds intensified and I fished out a pair of yellow expanding ear plugs to check the noise. The din is both a disturbance and a comfort. To the Iraqis, who have been bombed by air for almost five weeks it is only possible to imagine the sheer terror of it all. The cumulative effect of intense artillery fire can destroy the morale of even the most determined soldier. The destruction bulletin, though, seemed modest — 3 tanks destroyed, some others damaged, and several artillery positions hit. There was a long way to go. The plan was to reduce Iraqi assets in the grid reference closest to the British positions from 400 to 40, grinding Iraq down to only ten per cent of combat effectiveness before a single British soldier was committed to battle.

At dusk the flat crump of the shells was joined by the fiery yellow signature of the MLRS rockets, which, like a movie projector, sent a beam of light across the darkening sky. At the battalion's O group the atmosphere in Colonel Johnstone's tented headquarters had perceptibly shifted. There is now about us an element of excitement and inevitability. An intelligence report delivered in the deadpan brogue of Captain Dermot Fulton, the Arab-speaking intelligence officer only adds to the growing thrill. Allied jamming of Iraqi radio is said to have been so successful elements of its 48th infantry division were being forced to rely on couriers to pass information. The 31st infantry division have been ordered to hold their position for as long as possible in the face of coalition attack. Responsibility for chemical weapons has been delegated from corps to divisional command level. The 31st have been issued with Yugoslav respirators and one piece rubberised NBC suits, gloves, but no boots, and two Atrophine needles. Surely then, they are prepared to use these vile weapons. The 46th Infantry Brigade's armoured personnel carriers are in positions facing south and south west of us. It is part of the 12th Armoured Division, almost certain to be an early British target. It is though, thought to be one of the less capable outfits in the Iraqi line up, consisting of one mechanised infantry brigade, two armoured brigades and a single battalion of self propelled guns and three of towed artillery. The dog days of February were drawing to an end.

*Feb 18.* All the correspondents had been summoned to divisional headquarters to be briefed on The Plan. This was part of the army's promise to keep us informed and we had been assured that the briefing would give us three clear days before the ground war commenced. It meant a chance to catch up on some gossip and see how the other half lived. What luxury — soldiers were actually washing clothes, and not just washing them but steeping and rinsing them and giving them a final dunk for good measure. For those of us now restricted to a miserable 2 litres a day it was a sobering sight. As we walked passed a dobie, or washing detail, which looked more like a launderette, Jock, one of our drivers, sneered "Remfs". 'Rear-echelon mother fuckers' was the colourful phrase used by infanteers to describe those whose duties were strictly back room. Those even further back, in support at Jubail, or 'flip flop city', were unkindly dubbed 'ACRs' — air conditioned Remfs. This place though, had the feeling of a comfortable camp site. The correspondents, for example,headed by the redoubtable Kate Adie, shared a tent complete with beds, electric lights, and a team of young soldiers to draw their washing water. There was a cookhouse with three hot meals a day and Diamond One, the nerve centre of General Smith's team, complete with green plastic carpet. Charts, plans and map traces were spread all over the 'bird table', marked with red for enemy and blue for friendly forces. It was here that the General and his staff first began drawing up Britain's part in the liberation of Kuwait as long ago as December 27. It was no surprise to learn that the first UK division could have begun hostilities as early as January 31 without any particular penalty, but in a war of this sort, with overwhelming political overtones, delays were inevitable. As we arrived, the cunning plan we had come to study was lying in photo-copied bundles, 47 pages in each, ready for distribution to commanding officers. On the cover, a distinct emblem — crossed sabres above a palm tree, offset by a triangle bearing a rhinoceros. Desert Storm was about to become Desert Sabre. It was another snappy American name. After Britain's appalling Operation Granby, I wondered what ponderous name Whitehall would have saddled historians with if they had the chance to christen the next phase of the war.

General Smith was not able to give this briefing, and nor, more's the pity, was the man who conceived it, Norman Schwarzkopf. At first the British had been alarmed by this big, short tempered and demanding man. At 6ft.3ins, 17 stone, and bullnecked, Schwarzkopf was a soldier's soldier. Copiously decorated for his two tours of Vietnam, he won 3 silver stars, 3 bronze stars and two Purple Hearts, but his gruff appearance hid an intelligent and extremely able commander. Once asked by reporters what sort of leader he was, he replied: "I am magnificent." He knew too, that deception is the cardinal principle of warfare. Like a good boxer or quarter-back, a general knows the value of a well executed feint. A keen military historian, Schwarzkopf's favourite battle, as much for its deceit as its audacity, was Hannibal's victory over the Romans. But instead of elephants, the Allies were using loudspeakers that looked as if they had been liberated from a disco. With no satellites, a timid air force, and crude ground reconnaissance, the Iraqis had no real means of knowing what was going on. So their only method of analysing allied planning was signals intelligence. It was also the means to fool Saddam too. Ghost divisions were created to fill the desert where for weeks British and American troops had been dug in. While the US marines had imaginatively come up with 'Task Force Troy' after the Trojan horse, the British simulated the activities of a full brigade through a constant stream of busy radio traffic. Two hundred miles to the east the desert was dotted with dummy tanks and cardboard APCs to fool Bedouin spies while the loudspeakers were trundled into folds in the sand to blast out the signatures of Challengers and Warriors. It was not just entertainment. And it had masked our move last month and that of another 100,000 plus men west, to mass not on the Kuwaiti border but Iraq's. Saddam was encouraged to think that 7th Brigade were part of the US marines force, which had been their original task, while the 4th Brigade was the theatre reserve, still manoeuvering back there on the coast.

It seemed likely that the Iraqis had little idea of the weight of forces deployed against them or how those forces would move. Their intelligence, strategic judgment and ability to respond has consistently been poor. Saddam's great equalisers are low-tech, berms, oil-filled trenches and minefields. Their assumption is that the coalition forces are going to fight them the way the Iranians did — wave after human wave. The allied plan though, was to simply avoid them. It was to be a huge armoured left hook from the west while at the same time presenting such a broad front of operations it would be difficult for Saddam to know where the point of main effort would be. Away to our left the US 82nd Airborne and the French; to our right the Pan-Arab force, and beyond them the American Marines. This we were yet to find out, was another part of the deception. There would in fact, be no seaboard invasion. That, more than anything, was what Saddam was anticipating. The sheer violence of the plan — before the British moved there would be three hours of artillery barrage — 500 guns over a ten mile front giving the greatest concentration of fire power since the 2nd World War. So intense, the bombardment would change the landscape of enemy territory. There was also a built in stagger to the attack — again to add to the confusion. While the Americans set off on G day the British would be held back for a further 24 hours. What no one could say was just when G day was going to be.

The plan was to isolate and cut off the Iraqis inside Kuwait by coming from the one direction they least expected — behind them. It would, we were told, achieve the destruction of Saddam's army without the destruction of Kuwait. The intention was to achieve it as quickly and as cheaply as possible, but even as he outlined it, Colonel John Reith, General Smith's Chief of Staff cautioned that few plans survived the first battle. The British division would pass through breaches blown in Iraqi's sand fortifications, in a line of 6,800 vehicles at a speed of 10 kilometres an hour. It would take some nine hours and we would surely be the biggest and most tempting target of the war. If Iraq were going to use chemicals they would come during this manoeuvre.

While the briefing had been of enormous value it only added to our frustrations. The story of the plan would have to remain secret until after the war. We did though, persuade the army to allow us to write a holding piece, a popular journalistic method of combatting embargoes. This way the reporters can describe what will happen as though it had, and the army promised to release it to the world once the invasion had begun. For some reason they never did. There was still confusion among the troops though with radio broadcasting a quadrille of 'will we, won't we, go to war?' Even Christopher Hammerbeck warned: "Politicians have to realise you cannot keep soldiers at fever pitch indefinitely in the expectation of political settlement. We need a declared political signal — and soon."

The only signal I got was on my return to the Royal Scots B company was receiving both their 2nd anthrax jab and inoculation against bubonic plague. That was the awfulness of this lunatic Saddam — that he could dare to use a disease as vile as plague. I joined a line in the desert and rolled up the sleeve of my non-writing arm for the jabs. That night when Mike and I talked the plan over with Potter he remarked sardonically: "I think you will find it professionally stimulating."

*Feb 19*. After a hot day we had lazily strewn kit all around the Warrior, but even on this of all nights, the weather was as capricious as ever. Somewhere around 2 am. rain crashed against the CARM which sloped down from the vehicle to give the six of us a sleeping shelter. I awoke in an instant, dashing to drag gear into the dry. In the pitch darkness it was a risky journey, skirting trenches, a slumbering signaller and gunner and the comatose figure of Major Potter who always slept with his rifle on the outside because, he claimed, he was the lightest sleeper. He didn't even stir. I threw open the back of the vehicle pitching in the clothes and belongings I could find. Even the duty soldier — each company ran stags or staggered duties of one hour throughout the night manning the radio — hadn't heard the rain, which by now was beating against the steel turret like hammer blows. Across the horizon was beginning an artillery barrage of extraordinary ferocity, matched by the powerful storm they thundered in unison. There was nothing to separate the flash of lightning from the yellow burst of cannon fire and the frightening roar of exploding shells from thunder. If there ever could be a vision of hell this was truly it. As I plunged into my sleeping bag to shut the awfulness of the din out, I began to laugh — this was my birthday.

At first light the extent of the storm was evident — clothes I had laboriously washed the day before lay in soggy heaps, trenches were ankle deep in water, and the ground was like marshland. Nights like the last can have a tremendous impact upon confidence. The uninitiated like Mike Moore and myself were almost depressed. Wet and cold, we were snappy and argumentative. Soldiers who are used to spending their winter nights on the Brecon Beacons, Catterick or Soltau in Germany, were much more relaxed and even tempered. My mood was not helped by the jag on my arm which had turned an ugly red and was making my head swim. But there was after all, some natural justice. Out of nowhere a shower detail had arrived for the men of A and B companies. Potter who was as dirty as the rest of us showed a lofty disdain, waving us off with the promise that he would not shower until the war was won. Norman Soutar displayed similar sentiments. "Once you've gone six weeks without running water another couple of weeks isn't going to make much difference," he reassured. As it turned out, neither Mike nor I actually got our showers as the event became a story we both wanted to record rather than experience. For the soldiers who joyfully scrubbed down it was an uplifting moment, giving a wonderful sense of well-being.

Later, Major Julian James who as brigade chief of staff, is Hammerbeck's right hand man, dropped by. As a staff officer he is viewed with a healthy disregard by the fighting soldiers. To Potter all staff men are 'nobs'. But Major James most definitely was not. The son of a Chelsea vicar he had fought as a mortar platoon commander during the Falklands with 3 Para. Of all the Army's regiments, perhaps, with the exception of the Ghurkas, the Paras had felt particularly disappointed not to be invited to fight in the Gulf. Back in Aldershot they were airing their grievances on T-shirts, after countless enquiries from well-meaning members of the public. On the front of the shirts were the words: "Yes, I am in the Paras" while on the back: "No, I'm not in the fucking Gulf." Cynicism is the Paras' stock in trade. I had just received a letter from a friend, Alan Lewis in Belfast, detailing 3 Paras Christmas Party at Palace Barracks at Hollywood. Alan had written: "On the wall of the dining hall was a reference (subtle) to a joy riding incident in Andersonstown, when two joy riders were stiffed in slightly dubious circumstances. The Paras had made a life sized cardboard cut out of a Vauxhall Astra, painted accurately in dark metallic blue. The whole car was stuck up on a wall in such a way that the two tailor's dummies at the front were giving the display a 3-D effect. The tomato ketchup oozing and bullet ridden door were the finishing touches. A large sign beside the door said 'Vauxhall Astra — built by robots, driven by morons, stopped by A Company'."

Captain Irvine and Gunner Page dropped by with some mail which included several birthday parcels, one from Fortnum and Mason. Some foie gras, a whole tinned partridge and olives. Did people at home really think we sipped dry martinis in the Officers Mess as the sun went down? I had lost count altogether of the tubes of sun cream which had arrived when what we really needed were vests and woolly socks. Today's delivery even included a 'cool stick' which you apparently dab on the forehead to reduce the temperature. We laughed over this as we shivered in the icy wind. There was also something new to read — an amusing if fanciful account of life on Britain's top selling newspaper — The Sun, called 'Stick it up your Punter.' Six weeks or so had intensified the feeling of belonging to a special sort of family. Tales from Fleet Street suddenly began to seem a long way away.

At work in the office

# DESERT WARRIOR

The wariness of the Royal Scots seems to have finally got through to our minder. He has reluctantly knocked the windscreen from his Land Rover as Colonel Johnstone has demanded. As the wind whipped up the sand you could see why he wasn't particularly happy about it. There were two final birthday surprises. Potter cooked a wonderful chicken curry and Mike Moore bought us each an American cot.

This article appeared in the Daily Mail Feb 19:

It began as a night to forget and ended as a day to remember. It was, in the scale of things, a pretty small event — but to me it was a minor milestone. A birthday in war time.

Almost 40 days into desert life, and of course you recall the familiar faces and voices of home. On a day like this you miss them terribly. But the company of men in time of war is something which, while not compensating for the absence of family and loved ones, goes some way towards it. It's what our parents' generation talked about and, frankly, something I never really believed. Ask a soldier here who he is fighting for and he will tell you Queen and country. Scratch a little deeper and you discover he is fighting for his friends. Compressed into the back of a Warrior armoured personnel carrier for your waking moments and sleeping in its shadow puts that camaraderie into perspective.

The night before, the Allies had put up an artillery barrage of extraordinary ferocity matched by chance by a powerful storm that thundered in unison. The sky looked as though a giant electrical circuit had run amok. While shellfire, rockets and lightning exploded overhead, wind and rain lashed down. From our side it was a picture of hell, and we could only imagine the awfulness of it to the Iraqi conscripts in their trenches a few miles from us over the sands. The reaction is to slide deeper into your sleeping bag and, instead of thinking of the similar pounding we too will soon face, fill your mind with home.

This night especially, it triggered a date and place and a person. A favourite table in a special restaurant where you could see the river even on the greyest of February days. I could see it with brilliant clarity. A glass or two of champagne and later a stroll along the towpath, perhaps dropping in at a riverside pub. It promised to be a wonderful day.

Suddenly, reveille ended the daydream. We stumbled sleepily into the Warrior for the 30 minutes of compulsory stand to. At first light the extent of the night's storm was apparent. Kit lay in soggy heaps, clothes washed the day before with the meagre water allowance were filthy all over again. Each man with the Royal Scots battle group is allowed half a gallon a day to drink, wash in and rinse T-shirt and fatigues. So when the radio crackled into life offering B company a shower detail a cheer broke the dawn stillness. With the desert as our bed we are all dirty. Some haven't seen running water for seven weeks and we clamber aboard a half-ton truck like a pack of grinning urchins. The showers are clean and the water plentiful. It is even possible to forget briefly an arm swollen and bruised after inoculation against another of Saddam's noxious gases.

Afterwards it was like an infusion of well-being. In years ahead I'll probably never believe that I once greeted an Army field shower as a birthday treat. But it goes some way to explain the whole extraordinary world out here — a world joined in haste with little thought for the experience to come.

At first the soldiers assumed that correspondents *had* to be there. When they learn it's a voluntary posting it has a strange impact. First it stops them in their tracks, then they shake with laughter. The first time it's unnerving. A little later you are laughing too.

Now platoons are being told to tear up letters from home. In the event of capture nothing must be found, no photograph of a sweetheart, nor scribbled message of love. To an enemy like Iraq, mail can be a powerful weapon to destroy the will of a prisoner. There are no exceptions. You are stripped of your non-combatant status very quickly.

It is dusk now, and around the diamond-shaped encampment the evening meal is being prepared. the morning's memory of home floats back, then suddenly it fades. Major John Potter, beaming all over his face, holds out a grenade tin. The smell of good food is irresistible. Not processed, ration food but fresh chicken rich with herbs and spices, a tub of exotic Fortnum's pate which has been lying at the bottom of a backpack for a rainy day and a can of non-alcoholic near-beer. It was a feast and I shall never forget the birthday I spent with the Desert Rats.

*Feb 20.* There was a widespread feeling that G day was only hours away. Certainly Norman Schwarzkopf favoured February

21 and it also squared with General Smith's promise to brief the correspondents three days before the ground offensive began. Now, on the very brink of the decisive movement, Mikhail Gorbachev was making a last attempt to broker a peace. None of us were terribly optimistic. We received our desert pattern NBC suits. These were for front line infantry only and, of course, their travelling companions.They were jealously coveted by the soldiers, not least to further the gulf between them and the Remfs. Body armour too had been redistributed, taken literally off the backs of the support troops, who strutted around in the stuff back in Jubail, while the men who really needed it went without. Now you could spot a Remf at a thousand paces — not only did he carry either an ageing FLN rifle or Sterling sub-machine gun but in his European issue disruptive pattern NBC suit, he stuck out like a sore thumb. Company Quartermasters had also begun delivering glint tape to ensure that the reverse V the allies had chosen as a universal symbol of friendly force (Arabic for the number 8) was visible at night. With understandable concern of being accidentally struck by one's own side, the tank and Warrior crews marked their vehicles with liberal quantities of the stuff. Fluorescent orange panels principally, to warn allied pilots were also fixed to turrets. Mike Moore whose cameras had withstood vast quantities of desert dust thanks to regular visits to an air jet administered by a REME sergeant, started to seal up his Nikons with camouflage tape. It not only helped to keep out the sand but also reduced the risk of glare. While Potter whose French-Canadian wife, Brigitte, had sent him a baby's toy bear as a reminder that she was expecting their first child in under two months, wrapped the whole thing in air-tight plastic — its very own NBC suit.

*Feb 21.* Gorbachev's intervention seems to have put the ground war on hold. All correspondents were summoned to divisional headquarters again to be briefed on what we could say and when. To date, we had all more or less embraced the Army's ground rules. They were reasonable, practical, but above all sensible. What Colonel John King and Lt. Col. Chris Sexton were now proposing was a kind of embargo on the war altogether, with some rigid and quite unnecessary restrictions. We would not be able to report the British invasion of Iraq, which after all would be a full 24 hours after the

Americans had gone in, yet we knew that our colleagues, the so-called unilaterals, and paid up members of the Rufty Tufty Club, would be doing their darndest to report the war, if not from right behind the US and British lines then from the more accommodating Arab units. There would be no compunction on them to observe any embargo, while we, the people who actually knew what was going on, would have to remain silent. We all appreciated the need for operational security but we were further told that details of where we would be reporting from would also be deliberately muddied. Thus my dateline would become, 'From Richard Kay with the Desert Rats in Iraqi held territory'. But perhaps most astonishing of all, we were no longer to refer to any of the battalions of the British division by name. Did Army intelligence surely believe that in the middle of the 'Mother of all Battles', Saddam would have a man nip down to the corner shop scouring the Daily Mail for news of the Royal Scots and Life Guards when he already had half a million men advancing towards him anyway. It seems he did. We could refer to

The author, middle back with Mike Moore to his right and the crew of Oscar Bravo. John Potter, kneeling left, holds a captured AK47

officers and men by name but never their units. So Major James Hewitt was simply the commander of a tank squadron, attached to the British armoured division. While it seemed fatuous it also seemed a disappointment to the soldiers. Suddenly now that war was about to start the regiments that everyone had been following back home were to become anonymous.

Other safeguards were to be built into our reporting too. We were of course, free to give accounts of setbacks should there be any, but descriptions of reverses could be subjective. For example, Colonel King told me: "You might think 100 casualties among the Royal Scots was very high, but in the greater scheme of the land battle that number might be very small indeed." But that seemed to me to be the point of locating journalists with battle groups. We were not here to report the big picture but the small one. There was also debate about the plan on which we had so meticulously been briefed. The Army view was that it was 'background' to put the whole operation into perspective. Well that was all right up to a point, but because of their embargo it would rapidly become irrelevant — old news overtaken by events. They finally agreed that we could produce stories in advance, minus particular details which they would then release at their discretion. It was clearly going to be a very rapid war. Mike Gouldstone for one, was betting on 72 hours, and he's a soldier. It would mean there was every chance we would get to run no film or copy out before hostilities ceased. To my certain knowledge the lengthy piece I submitted to be released once action was under way, never reached London. It was to be immensely frustrating because the early accounts we picked up from radio were so larded with second guesses, estimates and inaccuracies, as to be positively misleading.

*Feb 22.* Brigadier Hammerbeck, who more than most perhaps, appreciated the advantages of an attentive press, is determined that every effort should be made to ensure his MRT get their stuff out. His plan is for an ageing and rather vulnerable 432 personnel carrier to be switched from operational resources to copy collection. He proposed that on day one the vehicle would circumnavigate the desert receiving film and copy from Mike Moore and myself with the Royal Scots, before trundling on to pick up Robert Fox's efforts with the 14th/20th King's Hussars, Simon Clifford's with the

Queen's Company, and Paul Davies and Nigel Thompson's ITN film from the Fusiliers. It would be a once only offer. If you were not ready the 432 had orders to move on to the next location. Gouldstone and the minders though were sceptical and generously, as it turned out, promised to stick to their tried and tested system as well. For us, saddled with an officer who appeared not have progressed beyond the orienteering kindergarten class, it did at least provide a second track.

*Feb 23.* In the darkness before the dawn the Siberian cold made you gasp. It was like opening the door of a butcher's freezer, and the wind was like a razor, slashing at your face. Over my tunic but beneath the body armour I put on an extra sweater, my last concession to civilian status. Padre Blakey, a committed Christian who despite his faith, saw a right in waging war, had wrapped a black and white checkered shermagh right around his neck and was handing out prayer books. Before him a trestle table covered with a tartan rug and a travelling kit of sacraments. Deal cross and silver communion cup, and standing beyond Royal Scots headquarters staff of 200 men, silhouetted in an orange glow from a fiery sun that was rising to replace the sight of the ugly angry flashes from the distant artillery. This was to be the last religious gathering. Together they said their regimental collect, but few shut their eyes, and this time the hymn singing was mute. When it was over, Iain Johnstone, who had been standing stiffly at the back, ordered the men to turn around. It seemed appropriate that after hearing God's word they should have their backs to the makeshift altar to listen to what their Colonel had to say. His message was about killing. Short, sharp, to the point, and very chilling. Unless the Iraqis had their hands up and wanted to surrender, they should be killed, he said. It was a policy to be pursued with absolute prejudice. If it couldn't be achieved with air strikes, artillery or cannon fire, then use your rifle, he said. The bayonet was the last resort. Now the Jocks had been sharpening the tips of these ferocious blades for weeks and told each other gruesome jokes of how many Iraqi ears they would need for a necklace.

Captain Irvine had orders to drive us over to Brigade Headquarters where Brigadier Hammerbeck was preparing to lead the Harbour party north to the assembly area from which the invasion will be launched. There was a brisk efficiency about him as he fussed around his tank for a final photo call, and he had some words of reassurance for his soldiers. "I know there are a lot of frightened young men out here, but they will do what they have to do. We are an extraordinary race and there is a casual humour to the British soldier that is a wonderful palliative to the strain," he said. "Anyone who holds the Queen's commission is going to feel very privileged indeed leading these men into battle." Of the plan, he said it was brilliant and inventive and would catch the Iraqis by surprise. Asked if he had any reservations about invading Iraq he was unequivocal. "We are going in to kick them out of Kuwait and the only way to unhinge their defence is by going round it and that means going into Iraq. I always said this ground war was inevitable." On his final morning of peace he had, he said, made a final peace with God too, by saying a Mass. He quipped: "I am totally bullet proof now because I have so many holy gismos." A reference to the dozens of letters, stuffed with talismans that had come to him from around the world. "I don't think one could go to war in better spirits. I cannot recall the British army being better supported by the public in history. We feel loved, wanted, and we jolly well are not going to let anyone down." He would attack the enemy in a cascading formation, one battle group after another. It would be, he said, "a beautiful, neat battle."

When we returned to B company the Padre was unloading ration boxes of American MREs. He was the Arthur Daly of the desert, a man who could prosper from any exchange and as skilled a negotiator as the company quartermaster. The 'quartie' had brought something for me too — an American issue anorak. OK, so it was woodland pattern, but it was warm and waterproof. While some Warriors were being loaded with supplies those with facines, for example, had stuffed bottles of mineral water into the pipes. Potter was being more realistic. He had instructed his section to load enough food and water for each man for five days.

He had something else occupying his time too, supervising the ammunition re-supply which was on such a scale that each Warrior resembled a mobile arms dump. "Any direct hit and these little babies are going to put on a firework display like you've never seen before," he liked to say. There were cases of hesh and tungsten tipped rounds for the 30 mm Rarden canon, belts of machine gun

Capture: in the aftermath of battle Iraqi prisoners are spreadeagled on the ground

Mutla Ridge: the carnage and the chaos. No one knows how many died here

bullets and boxes of grenades. Every infantryman has his favourite weapon. Potter's undoubtedly was the unfamiliar but potentially devastating rifle fired close assault weapon, or CLAW. Fitted to the end of the SA80, the French built CLAW is aimed and fired direct at a target 100 to 200 metres away. The warhead is supposed to arm 15 feet after it has left the rifle's barrel. It was designed to take all the risk of exposure out of pitching a grenade combined with a far higher degree of accuracy. "We're going to use a lot of these," the Major confided. With so many munitions inside the Warrior, compromising what little space there was, we had to move food supplies outside. A discarded Milan missile crate was lashed to the side and loaded with water and MREs.

That evening there were more letters and parcels from home. It seemed extraordinary that with conflict probably only hours away the Army were still able to devote men and time to the sorting and delivery of mail. Yet 4th Brigade has ten members of the Postal and Courier Regiment tasked only to distribute 3,000 letters and packages, which are driven up to the front by the lorry load from Jubail every day. I remembered that Warrant Officer Colin Stables had told me: "Mail is crucial to morale, with no access to telephones the letters to and from home are vital." Most soldiers had been writing daily but some had been sending between 15 and 20 letters out each day. I was beginning to receive letters from readers, some forwarded by the Mail, others addressed directly to me in the desert. I couldn't help but feel humbled. One from a soldier's mother had been especially moving. Quoting her son Phil, she wrote: "lots of politicians talk rot — John Prescott. For news about the Gulf I like articles by Richard Kay. His information is quite accurate although he does make it a bit sensational. Mind you, he manages to make me feel proud of what I'm doing out here. Maybe thats why I like reading his columns. Successful journalism?"

*Feb 24.* At stand to at 6 am. Major Potter had a brief announcement. The Ground War had begun two hours ago. As soon as we were able to open the Warrior's doors to admit the dawn at 6.30 we switched the radio from channel to channel to keep up with the rapid developments. The Marines and Arab forces were invading in the east, while in the west the French 6th Light Armoured Division and the 82nd Airborne set off like a high speed train in the headlong rush to seize Salman Air Base. The 82nd was the unit which parachuted into Normandy at the start of the D-Day landings. When General Maurice Schmitt, France's senior commander visited US units in the desert, they raised a banner bearing the words "Welcome General to Saint Mere l'Eglise," the village behind Omaha beach where the 82nd landed in June 1944. The Iraqis though are said to be fighting well, until the Allies close air support arrives, then they are giving up. Outside it was a terrible day. Dust storms drove across the desert, bringing the promise of rain. Already in those early hours the inaccuracies we had warned the Army about were evident in the radio reports. British troops, the World Service said, had pushed well into Iraq, accurately detailing our position but ignorant of the fact that our move was still 24 hours away, although the speed of the assault was to change all that. Soldiers stood in knots, unwilling to stray far from the security of their Warriors, idly checking weapons and talking little. After several hours with broadcasts even on the World Service preposterously talking about the 'Great British Advance', many began snapping off radios with impatience. It seems they are viewing the progress of the Americans and French with a mix of pressure and envy. "They had better leave some Iraqis for us," was a frequent grumble or: "If they haven't been caught they will probably have legged it by the time we start."

Just after 11 am. Potter fished out a blue and white St. Andrew's flag, which he fixed to the rat's tails, the three fluttering rags which together with the twin aerials, designated his command vehicle. Others were attaching the yellow lions rampant, and the desert began to resemble a medieval encampment. Rain was slicing across the landscape now, and the ground was becoming heavy, and I began to wonder just what battle was going to be like. So many guns firing, planes filling the skies, troops with bayonets, but with trenches and wet sand too, could it really be like July 1916 when Britain suffered 60,000 casualties on the first day of the Battle of the Somme? Certainly that was what Saddam appeared to want. I did though, take enormous comfort from being surrounded by such high quality soldiers and officers, many of whom in only a few weeks, had become firm friends.

Some of the older men washed and changed their fatigues, knowing that if they were hit they stood less chance of getting gangrene infection if clean cloth was forced into the wound. Major

Potter was silent, and as wrapped in his thoughts as I had ever seen him. I asked him how he felt and he was brutally honest. "I feel very lonely," he said. "I have complete confidence in the men to do what is required of them, but at the same time I am the man responsible for their lives — all 165 of them." There is no doubt he is a man who enjoys the responsibility of leadership, who will by example treat the Iraqis fairly, but his compassion for some of God's other creatures, is less certain. As the three of us stood kicking up clouds of sand into the wind, Private Watt, a muscular but gentle giant, bounded up with his hands clamped together and said: "Look sir, look what I've found." Gingerly opening them he revealed a four inch long sand lizard. Without a word Potter had his bayonet in his hand. There was a flash of steel and the unfortunate reptile was decapitated. If Mike and I were astonished it was only because it seemed so out of character.

A bigger surprise was to arrive in the shape of crop-haired Corporal Ray Thompson. We were to get an additional travelling companion. The Corporal, whose job was to take charge of the Warrior

Blinking into the daylight: Mike and me after 48 hours 'banged up' inside the Warrior

once Potter dismounted, must have wondered why Mike and I looked so appalled at his arrival. It was simple really. The two of us had established a kind of routine in the back of the vehicle. I shared the tiny fold-away table with the radio operator Corporal Gilchrist, while Mike had twin seats;the one on which he balanced his camera gear, was in fact a commode. Beneath its hinged flap it also held the Heath Robinson like tubes of the Beresford Flask, a complete if inconvenient convenience. Now we found our whole space compromised and our routine disrupted.

There had been a sea-change in Captain Irvine when he came by to see us that afternoon, our last lunch time rendezvous before action. There was a steely professionalism about him. He and Page had loaded crates of hand grenades into the Land Rover. Four were right  there on the dash board, ready to be hurled through the empty windscreen. Boxes of mineral water and compo packs were stuffed into every inch of space. After all the difficulties between us, he offered Mike and I a rather stiff handshake and promised not to let us down, that he was determined to get our copy through. "I won't fail you," he said. When the fighting began his was going to be a highly dangerous mission. Not only was he especially exposed in a soft skinned vehicle — there was no armour plating on a Land Rover — but he would be travelling against the advance. The so called 'Red Ball Express' — the American nickname for the column of advancing armour — would be moving on eight carefully marked lanes, four for track and four for wheeled vehicles. It was to be a one-way street affair. Anyone coming in the opposite direction could quite reasonably be treated as enemy. So not only was there risk from our own guns, the advance was planned to be so swift it was inevitable that pockets of Iraqi resistance would be left behind. A tank or two or company of soldiers bypassed in their revetments would, quite naturally, seek out the softer easier targets of the truck convoy, following well behind the armoured advance. I learned later that Captain Irvine had received some last minute navigation training from Mike Gouldstone, but more than that he had appealed to his professionalism and pride.

Captain Alex Alderson, Potter's second in command, retained a great sense of humour despite suffering terribly from piles. He was also keen to articulate many of the soldiers feelings. Only when the first shots are fired will we know how all of us will react, he would frequently say. He was right. What has been especially peculiar about the war so far is that we have not experienced a single air raid, artillery bombardment, or even sniper fire. Our 6 ft. deep trenches have been used as nothing more than a repository for sweet wrappers. Even the dreaded chemicals for which we had steeled ourselves for so long seem less of a threat than, say, a month ago. Colonel Johnstone's words of prosecuting this affair with extreme prejudice has not been lost on the Jocks. "We don't want to kill them, but we will kill them," is the usual response to questions. But one soldier, speaking with a little more candour said: "Most of us would say that 20,000 dead Iraqis is not enough. Every soldier we lose is going to get our blood up. We won't be able to kill enough of them. There are two parts to what we have to do — kill people, and survive." Gunnery Captain Tom Watson, 23 years in the army who earned his commission the hard way rising through the ranks, argued that the main fear coursing through the men would be the fear of failure. "They don't want to let their mates down," he said.

At 3.30 pm. Potter has been briefed to prepare to move. The allies themselves have been taken by surprise at the swiftness of the advance. The breathtaking speed encouraged Schwarzkopf to bring forward the timing of the attack by the 'big boys', the heavy armour, which included the British division. We are ordered into our new desert issue NBC suits when abruptly Major Potter explodes. His cherished satellite navigation system has gone down. A REME section hastily fits a new one and at 3.45 the company moves on Route Yellow, to the staging area. The British attack has been brought forward 15 hours and after 4 hours manoeuvering amid massive congestion we arrive only a few miles short of the Iraqi border berms. Fuel bowsers sweep down the lines of Challengers and Warriors, an operation that goes on long after nightfall. B Company is parked in long single file behind James Hewitt's tanks. Four hundred yards across the sands to our right Norman Soutar has lined up A Company and beyond them the pennants of Colonel Johnstone's tactical headquarters. The barrels of the big Challengers point directly ahead to the Iraqi lines. Major Potter instructs shell scrapes to be dug and the sand or dib-dibbah as the ordnance maps refer to it as, is thankfully soft and compliant. Two feet down it provides protection from artillery shrapnel but not much more.

We start on the Padre's box of American rations, the MREs. Each brown plastic envelope contains a packet meal that simply requires heating up in the Bee Vee, a slab of fruitcake, waterproof matches, chewing gum, and about 3 sheets of toilet paper. In the blacked out darkness of the Warrior each meal is something of a lottery. Chicken a la King, or Spaghetti Bolognese. Yet strangely in those hours before going to war, there is almost trivial concern as we argue over our choices for food.

*Feb 25.* At dawn the weather had turned even fouller. Thick cloud skated menacingly across the horizon, driving rain in bursts as ferocious as any tropical storm. Scanning the slate sky even Major Potter, an eternal optimist, conceded that our guardian angels of A10s and F15s were unlikely to be able to fly. They'd be grounded by weather. Colonel Johnstone has summoned his battle group commanders for a final briefing at 8.am. We are all in NBC suits and rubber over-boots. None are tailored couture, but the Colonel's seems especially ill fitting and uncomfortable. Not surprising really, as he confides that an accident during a night-time call of nature meant he had to hack off the braces that held up his trousers. Sipping a chipped plastic beaker of coffee, which he liberally passes around, he is though, as competent as ever. "Gentlemen", he says "this will be the last time we meet until we have achieved our first objective and reorganised." The battle groups orders have been confirmed. Although General Smith has finally decided that 7th Brigade should be first through the breach, an honour we all conceded they deserved because they had been in the desert considerably longer, the Royal Scots would almost certainly be encountering the first Iraqi resistance. There is enormous pride that the Jocks have been entrusted to take on the 46th Mechanised Brigade which despite round the clock air raids and savage artillery bombardment, is still assessed as 50% combat effectivess. There is also professional satisfaction that the Royal Regiment of Fusiliers on the other hand, has orders to deal with what is thought to be an Iraqi chemical stock pile. "Sappers work," sniff the Jocks. It also compensated for my own professional disappointment at being deprived of the dateline of the first reporter inside Iraq.

There were no new traces to add to the charts the officers already possessed of Objective Brass, but an intelligence report that the area had once been subjected to seismic tests which could give the appearance of minefields. "We should still remain prudent", said the Colonel. His officers sat on their helmets or webbing packs, their faces already lined with tension, fidgeting with the charts they had rolled out on their knees. They knew the plan backwards. From behind the tanks of the 14th/20th, the Life Guards leading, B company and A company following would sweep north, across the oiled road, turn hard right and race straight into the Iraqi position from the one direction they least suspected — their behind.

Prudence was the word of the day, not only in dealing with Iraq's minefields, but also with those created by the Allies. American planes had dropped thousands of time delayed bomblets which could take off a man's leg. At all costs when outside the vehicles we were to move only in their tracks. The Colonel again warned of the dangers of Iraqis booby-trapping both themselves and kit temptingly left lying around. "We are getting lots of reports of Americans being horribly injured by picking up trophies like map cases and rifles. If you want to have a look at anything, get a prisoner to bring it to you," he said. "You must stop the soldiers from being curious, otherwise they will lose limbs." All abandoned enemy vehicles were to be disabled, their weapons destroyed, while any Iraqi dead would be treated with respect, their bodies buried and the graves recorded so that they can be repatriated for burial at home later. The invasion, he said, was going extremely well but he cautioned against complacency. The US had halted their advance the previous night either because of the risk of fratricide after last light, or to add to the Iraqi confusion as to where the main effort was coming. It seemed they were still convinced the assault would be full frontal, up the Wadi Al Batin, the only natural depression in the western desert and the border between Iraq, Kuwait and Saudi Arabia. Johnstone had few final words but they were hugely prophetic. "I don't think this is going to be that difficult, but I don't want people to be stuck in trench clearance. Either the enemy surrenders or we kill them."

The hours that followed moved painfully slowly. I walked along the lines of the Life Guards watchful tanks, the flash of cigarette in cupped hands were like fireflies against the gloom. Lt. James Gaselee's troop were playing three card brag, and betting blind. The pot contained bundles of Saudi riyals, water money the boys said they wouldn't need any more. But the playful boasts belied their nerves. As the hours dragged by some soldiers read, mostly back copies of the satirical comic Viz, others tried writing last letters home which they would leave with their commanding officers in the event of tragedy. I was frequently shown them and encouraged to help them articulate their feelings for loved ones. As expert I had become it was difficult to avoid being over-sentimental, but the more mawkish I was the better these young men liked it. I have no idea how many households must have received such sloppy words.

Back at the Warrior I find the General, our Gunner Lance Corporal Jim Lee, bent in prayer, not for himself, nor even for the company, but for the men of 7th Brigade, who are crossing the border ahead of us. "They may be Pommies but God alone knows what's in store for those who encounter the Iraqis first," he says. At 1 pm. Potter receives orders that the company is on immediate notice to move. CARM nets are quickly hauled down and stowed. Gash pits, which once we had carefully concealed, are barely touched. It no longer seems to matter. Thirty two minutes later the company begins to move forward. Potter's final telegraphed words "Zero Bravo (his call sign) we are moving now."

The radio operator, Ben Gilchrist, had fixed up a head set so that I could listen to both the company and battle group network The radio crackles with static, expletives and tension. The Life Guards had raced ahead. "Those fucking tankies are going too fast." At 4 pm. we pass a newly dug grave. It has been marked with a cross, a sheet of chemical resistant polythene, and the victim's boots. Whenever he could Potter would provide me with a running commentary, and frequently signal down for us to fling open the rear doors so Mike could exercise his itchy camera finger. It also brought in lung-fulls of fresh air. For in T-shirt, uniform, NBC suit and body armour, the Warrior was like a sauna. To our right and left are the Americans who have exploited Iraq's border defences, opening them up like a can, so that the Brits can pour through. The Americans punch the air and wave fists in salute as we pass them, and all around we witness the devastation caused by their assault. Heaps of destroyed Iraqi equipment, smouldering and useless, but frightening still in their jagged, black massiveness. Dead metal showing through the grey black smoke. Here the remains of a D 30 towed artillery piece, probably the victim of a direct hit by a cluster bomb. There a burned out tank, and near by a dismembered soldier. Extraordinary that these are the first corpses we have seen in the war. Two kilometres from the border and the sheer power of the bombardment is apparent. The vast sand berms which have been talked up so much we thought we would need grappling irons to scale them, have, like the walls of Jericho, come tumbling down. Those that survived the aerial attacks have simply been bulldozed aside. God knows how many must have perished here or even been buried alive.

The pace appears to be quickening, and at 4.42 pm. we cross into Iraq. For Mike and I it is a moment of supreme exhilaration. We exchange a grin, but even before it sinks in, Potter is on the radio with a witty announcement. "Gentlemen, we've got no time to stamp your passports, but then I don't think there is anyone to do it." Now there is an additional task to tonight's programme. Colonel Johnstone has received quick battle orders, or in army jargon "Quebec, Bravo, Oscar." 'Objective Bronze' a clear and destroy mission, had unexpectedly been passed to the Royal Scots. At last light, as the battle group assembles in its forming up position, or FUP, deep inside Iraq, senior officers are hastily summoned by the Colonel. It is a hazardous journey — the whole area is littered with mines and delay action bomblets, forcing us to leap down vehicle tracks like gymnasts. As the officers met, Warrior crews hurriedly refuel their vehicles from jerry cans, then at 6.10 pm. the first salvo of MLRSs roar over our heads into the suspected Iraqi artillery position we have to attack. It is an awesome sight and fills us all with an immense sense of power. I can see the rockets streak across the sky and feel the carpet of explosions that shakes the ground moments after. There had already been an air strike by A10s that had dodged the squalls and cloud cover and it is hard to think that anything or anyone would be left alive after all this.

As the H-hour of 7.30 pm. approached (it had been brought forward 30 minutes because of enemy movement) the Challengers and Warrior fighting vehicles switched on red identification tail lights. The rain now had got even harder. The combined effect for the tank and APC commanders was to considerably reduce the effectiveness of image intensification sights. As we waited, Potter received a report on the progress of the invasion which demonstrated its astonishing breadth. The Marines had attacked Kuwait airport, while the 'Screaming Eagles', the 101st Airborne, were in the Euphrates valley already, straddling Highway 8 just 150 miles from Baghdad. And Saddam still had to face the fury of the Royal Scots!

The General loaded three rounds of Sabo and three rounds of HE into the magazine of the Rarden gun with a practised flourish, checking and re-checking the calibration of the sights. I know that he wants to fire this gun in anger, and I know that I want him to, too. As we moved off the moustachioed Corporal Thompson pulled a picture of the fiancee he should have married on Valentine's Day from a breast pocket. For a moment he stared at the snapshot, smoothing its dogeared corners, then put it away, picked up a pencil and calmly opened a book of word puzzles. It was a process he was to repeat over the coming hours as tension and danger grew.

Gunning the Warrior forward, the driver, Private Les Watt, uttered four words before lapsing into silence that I don't think was broken until the war was over. "Here we fucking go," he said. Visibility which had been poor now became progressively worse. Over the headset I heard Captain Alderson who was behind mutter "I hope you have been eating your carrots." Potter, preoccupied with ensuring his call signs were remaining in battle configuration, appeared not to hear. Instead he asked for two aspirins to be handed through to him in the turret to counteract the pain of an old leg wound. Mike, who had spent hours polishing and blowing dust from the crevices of his cameras, has a resigned look on his face. It says "I can't take pictures in the dark." Within minutes our advance is a mess. A massive convoy, probably from 7th Brigade, has sliced right through the battle group and to compound it, the Life Guards have disappeared altogether. There was a further delay for US artillery support as the assault got further behind schedule. We had been travelling four hours covering just five kilometres an hour. Coupled with the heat inside the Warrior, the lack of progress had an extraordinary effect. It sent both Mike and me to sleep. Not for long. The headset was still clamped to my ears and Colonel Johnstone briskly informed Major Potter, "You're in a mine field." What would a mine do to us? I ventured. "They are probably only anti-personnel jobs, but they might blow a track off," he answered matter-of-factly. There was no evasive action to take — we just continued. Seven kilometres from the target and another salvo of rockets rained down on the Iraqis. Potter in his turret rotated constantly from left to right, scanning the blackness vividly illuminated through his thermal imager. At six minutes to midnight the reassuringly educated voice of James Hewitt comes over loud and clear. "We have strong thermal signatures to our front." Translated it meant the Iraqis were on the brow of the hill.

*Feb 26.* On Major Hewitt's order the 14 tanks of A squadron opened fire on the Iraqis at two minutes after midnight. The crash of their big 120 mm guns reverberated inside the Warrior as Potter manoeuvred his eyes, blinking into the inky darkness. Fighting in tanks and APCs is a remote affair, with hatches battened down the Commander must peer through sights, requiring immense powers of concentration. Hewitt though, makes it sound like an excursion with the Household Cavalry down Rotten Row. "We have engaged and destroyed approximately ten infanteers," he intones over the head set. "There is very light resistance. One or two pop up and fire a round and then get down again." The thought of the Iraqis, trapped in their trenches, as the tanks fire their massive shells, replying with small arms, already seems pitifully inadequate. The target is a bunker system and after repeated calls for rounds of 'illume', or flares, fails to materialise, Johnstone orders another rocket strike. Potter brings forward two platoons, parallel with the Life Guards, and their chain guns and cannon compete with the thud from the tanks. At 12.16 am Hewitt spots a figure waving a white flag and his tanks cease firing. At last flares are popping down everywhere, and Potter orders 5 Platoon to move in to take the surrender. "Don't stand for any monkey business," barked Johnstone, echoed in turn by Potter to the platoon commander, Lt. Alistair Stobie. "Proceed with absolute caution," he said before uttering "where are their fucking tanks?" The voice of the youthful Stobie, whose platoon I suppose is the cream of the company, crackles over the air: "I am going to fire a warning burst over their heads." But the slowness is frustrating the Colonel. "Get those people rounded up," he cuts in. Potter himself decides to take control, and suddenly our doors opened to admit the sight of battle. As the Major grabbed his SA80 and raced out into the darkness, another flare scoots into the air, throwing the scene into grotesque relief. Away to our left there is more fighting, and flames of orange and red, like a ruined star falling to earth. It is in fact A company attacking seven bunkers.

The tanks meanwhile, squat monstrous things, were crushing the Iraqi trenches out of shape, gun barrels swivelling around. The air was thick with cordite and red and white tracer stitched a pattern across the night sky. It was all horribly fascinating and I felt spellbound as I crouched in the protective shadow of the Warrior. Prisoners were appearing from nowhere. They were a pitiful sight, ill-shod, some were bare foot altogether, others in flip-flops. How could they hope to compete with a modern professional army? And yet at the same time I could not help thinking what curiously empty people the Iraqis seem to be. All this strutting and machismo when they invaded little Kuwait — bullies — but when it comes to a fight they hadn't got the stomach for it. God knows how they understood the guttural shouts of the Jocks, who circled menacingly. Few spoke English, but none needed to be told a second time and they hugged the wet sand gratefully. When one man, perhaps in his late thirties raised his head out of terror, he was bludgeoned down, not by a rifle butt nor even a boot, but the vocal power of a voice from the meaner streets of Edinburgh. Another prisoner was on his knees in front of Potter, grappling at his feet. He was trying to embrace him — saviour or executioner, he didn't seem to care. For a moment I thought John was going to shoot him but the man was trying to give him his surrender. He thrust upwards with a white cloth, covered with illustrations on how to dress a wound. It was a field dressing. "Christ," Potter said "I almost shot the poor bastard, and he only wanted to kiss me." Two Iraqis came from nowhere and humbled themselves in front of Mike Moore as he was squinting through his Nikon. Walking smartly back to the Warrior he airily announced: "I think someone with a gun had better come around here." But before anyone could move the two had followed Mike back, as pathetically as lost children. They were coming from all directions, some were sobbing, one was shrieking "I'm a Christian, don't shoot me. I love Jesus." A Lieutenant with two gold stars on his shoulder had been brought up to Potter. He was a big, clumsy man. In his hands he held a tattered white rag — he looked like he should have been a farmer but he spoke some English. An interrogation began. "Where are the tanks? Where are the senior officers? How many men?" It was a machine gun delivery, but in his anxiety to answer the Lieutenant was even quicker and his mouth outran his brain. We did learn however, that the senior officers had already deserted, instructing their men to surrender. Also there was another artillery position, 800 metres away. Of three guns there, two still survived.

Corporal Thompson meanwhile, had rifled the pockets of a three-star Captain. He laid out on the sand a pencil, a pile of brand new banknotes, and passed me a notebook of lined paper. On one page was the start of a letter, perhaps to a loved one. On another some multiplication, calculating wages possibly, and on a third, sketches of artillery gun positions. Another prisoner too, had been relieved of a bundle of banknotes, which someone suggested meant they must have recently been paid, although I supposed they could have been paid at any time. Where after all, could they spend it out here? Suddenly there was a yell from Potter "MINES!" The nipple-like trigger of an anti-personnel device only inches from the spread fingers of one of the prisoners was peeping through the sand. Thompson dragged him by the collar and demanded to know where the mines were. The man signalled hopelessly, circling his arm. We were in the middle of a minefield. Now every indentation in the sand resembled danger. Quickly Potter ordered them to be marked with green cylumes. The interruption had halted the company's advance, and with almost 50 prisoners the Sergeant Major and fitter section were tasked to muster them and move them back down the line. Most of them were lying face down behind Potter's Warrior. They seemed convinced they were going to die. We were now certain that those who had perished as the tanks began their advance on the position, had died because they were too frightened to get out of their trenches. Fearing being shot if they showed themselves they cowered in the bunkers that became their death traps. As the round-up continued I spoke to one private soldier who assumed he was the prisoner of the Israelis. "You have come from the west. You must be Israeli," he said. There was a logic to his assumption for he did not even know the British were fighting this war. "These are Scottish soldiers," I told him. "Will they kill me?" he asked. Potter appeared at my elbow and winking at me answered "No son, for you the war is over." Then turning to me said "I've always wanted to say that."

So many Iraqis apparently wanted him to say it that it was almost 3 am. before Potter was able to move the company forward to assault another series of bunkers. There was no doubting his genuine humanity and distaste for killing people whose only crime was a fear of surrendering, so he brought the forward elements of the company up to the rim of the trench system and instructed the Warriors to flash their headlights, to encourage the vanquished Iraqis to give in.

The expectation of an enemy counter-attack and the knowledge that at least one Iraqi artillery piece was still able to work contributed to the nervousness that we all now felt. The confusion was compounded by reports of a huge convoy moving ahead to the north of us, which intelligence insisted could only be an enemy one. After repeated assurances by Brigade Headquarters that there were no friendly forces in the area, the battle group swung north into a firing line to engage what appeared to be 50 armoured vehicles converging on the Royal Scots left flank. I don't know how close the tanks came to opening fire on this column. Certainly both James Hewitt and John Potter expressed reservation that this was an enemy convoy at all, and it's quite possible only a handful of seconds and a few nagging doubts prevented the battle group from destroying a British field hospital. Dressing Station 5 Alpha and its army of Ghurka ambulance men blithely continued their progress unaware of how close they were to annihilation.

Such was the congestion of armour in such a geographically small area, the risk of being attacked by one's own side was huge. Indeed later most soldiers confided that they were more concerned about being killed by "friendly fire," the army's offensively tactless term for accidental shooting, than by the Iraqis.

All trace of tiredness had washed away, such was the excitement, despite the apparent lulls between engagements. B Company was ordered to attack enemy bunkers at 3.05 am. but the task switched and it was first light, perhaps two hours later, before we made contact with a dug-in Iraqi infantry position. There was a rattle alongside the Warrior. It sounded like raindrops on a steel helmet. We had been hit. The Warrior lurched to a halt and Corporal Thompson was instructed outside to check the damage. As he gingerly opened the door there was a burst of machine gun fire and he promptly slammed it shut again. Not everyone it seems, wanted to surrender. The tanks closed, firing high explosive squash head shells and after a while Thompson reopened the doors. This time he had got his 'Handy Cam' video recorder in his hands, and assiduously began

filming the carnage. Here's a man, I thought, with no time for sentiment. The dead and injured were lying around on the wet sand,
those still alive distinguished by their soft moaning. Here the Iraqis,
disorientated and defeated, had been caught in the open. They were
the remnants of a mortar locating battery and they had made pathetic attempts to avoid the tanks by digging scrapes in the sand
with their hands. Another 21 prisoners lay face down. Again, you
had the feeling they were the lucky ones. Three more were horribly
wounded, cut to pieces with machine gun fire.

The company medic, Lance Corporal Brian Meechan, was called
forward and I watched with a feeling of pride as he gently treated
these men as if they were his brothers. Their injuries were very
serious. One with a sucking wound to the chest, another with shrapnel embedded in his shoulder. But the third had multiple wounds.
He had been hit eight times in the right leg, the bullets smashing his
tibia and fibia. Blood poured from the entry and exit wounds. Another bullet was lodged in the man's stomach. Amid all the mayhem
and gunfire, Corporal Meechan applied eleven separate field dressing — each one of which was able to hold a pint of blood — administered a phial of morphine and set up a drip. The casualty survived
and Meechan and his assistant, Private Blake, were singled out for
their courage. In the Company citation, Major Potter wrote: "There
is no doubt that Lance Corporal Meechan and Private Blake saved
the lives of the two seriously wounded EPWs (Enemy Prisoners of
War). That they worked under constant threat of enemy artillery
bombardment and counter attack is to be commended. Their professional approach and speed of treatment allowed the company to
move off as quickly as possible without hindering CO1RS's plan
(Commanding officer of the 1st Royal Scots), while fulfilling our
obligations under the Geneva Convention."

The look on the face of the young conscript as Meechan knelt
over him was of incomprehension. He couldn't believe that this
soldier, a man who took his orders from 'The Great Satan', was
saving his life. Meanwhile the Padre had come forward to officiate at
the burial of the dead. They were sprawled in the extravagant posture of men killed suddenly in battle. One had his face blown off,
another had a four inch hole in his chest, and a third had only a black
cavity where his chest should have been. In his meticulous log, Potter wrote against each victim "death instantaneous."

WAR

Among the prisoners were seven officers, one of whom spoke reasonable English claiming to have been at college in England. He grinned a lot, but it was not arrogance, rather the smile of relief. He was, he said, happy to be a prisoner of the British. He was holding a grubby satchel which he gave to me. Inside were three stale rolls and a packet of dates. The rations on which Saddam hoped to repel the armies of the alliance. Dishevelled and undernourished, it now seemed astonishing that these soldiers had been dubbed 'The Prussians of the Middle East'. It had taken four hours to clear the objective, and a rasp of impatience was clear in Colonel Johnstone's voice as he ordered the battle group to turn up for the main event. In an effort to get on, casualties were passed back in our own ambulances, indicating not only the urgency of pressing home the attack but also the confidence.

It was 8.11 am. when the Royal Scots finally embarked on the enemy position they had spent so long poring over — 'Objective Brass'. Two regiments of artillery pounded down 155 mm shells as A and B companies trekked for two miles behind the Life Guards Squadron. As the light had come up so the visibility had appeared to reduce through the combined effect of the bombardment and high winds. It was down to just 500 metres. The Iraqis were extremely well dug in, making in army jargon, 'target acquisition' very difficult. Once again we were sweeping behind James Hewitt's Challengers, who for the first time had some solid opposition, Soviet built T55 tanks. The appearance of enemy tanks galvanised Potter. The Warrior slammed into reverse thrust, pulling back as Hewitt's men engaged and destroyed four tanks. The desert was all churned up, and Potter ordered his mortar section which had targeted a bunker system , to cease firing. There was a sudden jolt, and the Warrior yawed violently to the left. We immediately feared we had hit a mine, but the vehicle carried on true. Someone had simply come too close with a glancing blow. Obscuration, was the word Potter grumbled repeatedly into his head set. What he meant was a real pea souper. Not fog of course, but the back draught of wind and war, driving sand, rain, smoke and fumes. He was desperately seeking his target, an Iraqi platoon with three MTLB personnel carriers. The company closed, destroying two of the APCs with their 30 mm cannon, but the third, thought to be a command post, was impervious to fire, concealed so deeply in a revetment.

Potter led the attack on the MTLB personally. It was to provide the most photographed piece of action from the ground war and brought a medal for a young private. The Major had already de-bussed 5 Platoon, when he instructed his signaller to join him outside the vehicle. I passed the two of them their SA80s which were snapped into racks at their feet, and with Mike Moore, clambered after them. Five prisoners already lay spread-eagled, but they were watchful of the scene that unfolded, as though they knew a surprise was in store. Anti-personnel mines were scattered on the ground like confetti; when one Iraqi insisted on pushing himself up to watch, Corporal Gilchrist, despite the burden of a radio back-pack, leapt across and waved his bayonet under the terrified man's nose. Under Sergeant Tom Gorrian, 5 Platoon had dashed towards the revetment. Gun fire sounded in every direction. Potter, Gilchrist and Mike Moore, zig-zagged their way across perhaps 100 yards of highly exposed terrain, the two soldiers ducking expertly. Moore, perhaps sensing his great opportunity, running effortlessly. As they arrived, Private Tom Gow 'on his own initiative,' as his citation was to later say, crawled to the rim of the crater, slotted a CLAW into his rifle barrel and, taking careful aim, squeezed the trigger. Instantly he followed it up by hurling in a white phosphorous grenade. More hand grenades followed and the MTLB exploded in a shower of bright shiny sparks, giving the gloomy scene a backlit effect. Two Iraqis emerged from the debris, their hands in the air. The rest had perished.

As the company reorganised, Captain Alderson's Warrior ran over a mine but, like the Iraqi soldiers, it was a dud. A metallic thud, a light lurch,and the vehicle was back on true. It was now 10.50 am. and the sound of battle had at last melted away. The action by the Royal Scots and Life Guards had destroyed six T55 tanks, 25 APCs, six anti-aircraft guns, 3 mortars, one artillery piece and yielded four score prisoners. In the stillness, the relief that we had not sustained a casualty was tangible. It was 30 hours since they had last slept and Johnstone ordered all vehicle commanders and drivers to snatch some sleep. For me there was no such luxury as I pulled out my typewriter to begin that first war despatch. Wind and rain were still rolling across the desert, making it impossible for me to work outside, and I sat with the Olivetti on my knees, as tired men around me grumbled about the din.

There was little time for creative thought and I was intent on writing the events of the previous 24 hours in a coherent style. But nothing of that first day and a half surprised me more than the arrival of David Irvine and Gunner Page, their faces pinched from the cold and wet that comes from peering into the darkness without a windscreen. They had taken considerable risks to reach us, negotiating mines and knots of bedraggled Iraqis, who instead of surrendering could have remained aggressive. It never occurred to me that the Captain would have been so prompt as to arrive before I was ready. He had also impressively outstripped Brigadier Hammerbeck's 432 which showed up hours later. Mike packaged his films and I crashed on pleading for 'just another few minutes'. After half an hour he was anxious to move. It was noon. Potter had been roused to be warned of an 'O Group' for the next battle. It was clear this was to remain a rapid and as decisive an advance as the generals had promised. Still unfinished, and protesting, I jumped into Irvine's Land Rover. It was at least two hours back to the drop off point where Mike Gouldstone would receive copy, before embarking himself on the even more hazardous drive to the transmission unit at Divisional Headquarters. I figured I could type in the back. I had forgotten though, how uncomfortable it was. As we pitched through bomb craters and the deep ruts of the tank tracks, correspondent and typewriter were more shaken than stirred. It was like being in a blender and impossible to work. Fortunately, Major Gouldstone, when we eventually found him, (Captain Irvine had thankfully got hold of a Magellan electronic way-finder in which you punched in the co-ordinates of the objective and it responded by telling you to adjust the wheel left or right, bringing you exactly to your destination), was in no position to set off. As surprised as we had been at Irvine's promptness, he said he could not leave for the FTU until the Division had "gone firm" themselves. I was therefore allowed another hour to polish the 1500 words I wanted sent, but by 3 pm., my minder, rightly concerned about the dangers of travelling after dark, insisted we set off back to the Jocks.

While ours was an uneventful journey, Gouldstone displayed exceptional bravery to get through with the copy. First he had to wait for the two other minders to drop off their despatches and it was nightfall before he could leave. Later he told me all about it. En route he ran into a rag-tag unit of lost, but still armed, Iraqis and

Gouldstone himself only carried a pistol, a 9 mm Browning — at less than 30 ft. about as effective as a pop-gun. But they only too willingly surrendered. One, who was badly wounded, gratefully draped himself over the Land Rover's bonnet, clinging to it for three hours without complaint as the Major altered his journey to hand his prisoners over to some Americans. The Iraqis were in fact no danger to him, but he was relieved when he came across the US group. He told them the wounded men needed urgent medical treatment, but the 'septics' were patronisingly indifferent as they told him they would take charge. A circle of guns pointed menacingly at the Iraqis, and Gouldstone left saddened by what he had seen. I later heard other accounts of unnecessary viciousness towards the Iraqis captured. As in other wars, it was clear that the further back the line from the action the more brutal was the treatment of prisoners. Certainly the Jocks accorded their POWs respect, the kind of respect that always exists between fighting soldiers — a sort of mutual admiration if you like. When Mike did arrive at General Smith's HQ the Evening Standard's Keith Dovkants, who largely spent the war selflessly transmitting other people's work was roused from his bed at about 1 am. He stood over the sensors and then spent the best part of two hours filing mine and Robert Fox's despatches, for he literally had to speak them down the telephone to copy takers at the Mail and Telegraph. In London the copy's arrival told different stories of Britain's newspapers. It was probably 2 am. in Kensington, but the Mail decided to put out an extra edition to run the report as well as releasing it to other newspapers as they were bound to do. The Telegraph though, suggested that the Mail might like to hold my stuff because they were not flexible enough to get Fox's piece in that morning's edition. My employers demurred, and it meant that we carried the first front line piece of British action. I was though, blessed, if that does not sound too uncharitable, for I do not mean to be, with the spectacular contribution of 7th Brigades MRT. All their copy was lost.

Meanwhile I rejoined the Royal Scots at dusk, in time to accompany Potter to his 5.15 pm 'O' group. What a difference from the last time I saw these men. Now their faces are blackened with soot and their uniforms stained with sweat, but the excitement in their red-rimmed eyes was still there as they pored over the plans to assault 8 positions in 'Objective Tungsten'. Quite simply they looked pleased with themselves as they had every right to. Johnstone's men had clearly impressed the high command for he announced that they were to receive an additional squadron of tanks for the new task. A squadron from the 14th/20th King's Hussars would be joining B company, while the Life Guards teamed up with A company. It was a confusing configuration.

As the Colonel briefed, a line of 70 Iraqi POWs appeared in the distance. They were jogging, or at least trying to. Many were so exhausted or unfit, shuffling would be a kinder description. One was lagging far behind, a huge Bunter-like conscript who, after every loping stride, found himself breathless. The Jocks roared at him to hurry up. It was almost comical, but there was a need for the haste for the prisoners were tying up resources and slowing down our progress. As darkness fell Potter passed on instructions to the company and I began to feel the fatigue of two days without sleep. The signal to move came at 8.pm. even though our armed escort from the Hussars had not turned up. Our route took us slap into the middle of another minefield. Wide awake now, I could feel every contour in the desert as driver, gunner and commander multiplied their tired eyes and squinted into the gloaming through their sights. It was 9.25 before that obstacle was behind us. There was now a long approach of some 30 kilometres, travelling through a number of friendly formations. One of the company Warriors had engine failure and was left behind. If it happened to ours, Potter said, he would simply commandeer his two ICs, the second in command's vehicle, and so on down through the company. The reconnaissance platoon of mobile but vulnerable armoured cars (sent ahead to negotiate a crossing over an oil pipe line which the Iraqis were using as a defensive breach), had already come under fire from enemy vehicles and the Colonel ordered an assault crossing.

*Feb 27.* At midnight Johnstone's voice crackled over the radio. This time he was launching Major Soutar's A company first, with B to come in on a flanking move. "So far it's apparent this enemy is going to fight. Be aware, don't be complacent," he said. The tank commanders were anxiously demanding a smoke screen for the assault over the pipeline. Their high profile meant that as the Challengers reared up to cross the obstruction, their bellies would be hugely exposed, and their was widely believed to be at least two squadrons of enemy T55s lurking beyond. A salvo of rockets screamed over us as Johnstone brought down a swift artillery barrage. Tired and with his leg providing much pain, Potter was not in the mood for running commentaries, confining his remarks to curses. The concentration of tanks and armour forced Johnstone to re-write the plan amid fears of inflicting damage to our own forces.Potter was concerned that he could not get an uncluttered line on an artillery position without the possibility of shooting up some of Soutar's men. It is hard to imagine the calm coolness of Colonel Johnstone, as man and machinery converged all around. But composed he remained as he directed Major Potter to attack a mechanised infantry company and an artillery battery. As the tanks scornfully blasted aside a handful of T55s, we streamed into a bunker system. Loaded with armour piercing shells the Warriors fired into revetments where the Iraqis concealed their guns and APCs. There was some sporadic return fire. A handful of RPG 7's, the rocket propelled grenade so loved by the Provisional IRA, were fired towards us, and Kalashnikovs spat out a few rounds. But within minutes the position was overrun. The surviving Iraqis and would-be prisoners were simply by-passed. There was also further concern over friendly fire, with the Royal Regiment of Fusiliers attacking on the battle group's southern flank. The Colonel was anxious to press on again.

Now each company was given the target of a tank squadron with Potter receiving additional instructions to destroy some armoured infantry too. As our Challengers appeared, the Iraqis legged it. When the moon set at 3 am. the only ambient light was from two burning T55 tanks which exploded periodically as ammunition detonated. With visibility down to 100 metres Potter instructed his mortar fire controller to launch flares to locate surrendering soldiers. None came. Johnstone called a halt, lining the battle group up, facing northwards. Over the radio he said, "Congratulations everyone. So far we have destroyed a Divisional Headquarters and a Brigade. Now eat and rest; let your commanders sleep." He warned: "We are on between two and four hours notice to move." Potter slumped gratefully in the turret, sleeping bolt upright, while Private Watt, the envy of us all now, with his bed-like seat, stretched out beneath his steering wheel. The rest of us we slumped inside. Mike Moore had anyway slept through much of the action while I had become expert at making brews, relieving Corporal Gilchrist of the chore during the night. But with no infantry action the pair of us were anxious to get out and look for stories.

Before dropping off to sleep Potter had got on the radio asking the adjutant to contact our minder so that he could drive us back over the battlefield, the scene of the previous night's fighting. It would give us the chance to see the scale of the attack and examine Iraqi trenches. With the second night without sleep, Captain Irvine too looked shattered when he arrived, but we raced off in the direction of a burning tank. On the way we picked up some extra muscle in the shape of a fearsome looking private soldier, who led the way with me.

This was a desolate place, high and windswept. There was evidence too, that far from being the well organised, disciplined army we had been told about, the Iraqis were closer to a rabble. We were especially curious to see the bunkers where so many soldiers had been living for nine months at least. Certainly those for the ordinary soldiers were hopeless, grim shelters, rancid even, with the putrid smell of decay. Their beds were wooden doors strewn with hessian sacking. The officers quarters though were surprisingly comfortable. One even had an elaborate vitreous china free-standing bathroom sink, complete with faucets and vanity suite. There were comfortable, if ageing pieces of furniture; pictures of pin-ups along with the inevitable portraits of Saddam, and bottles of cheap cologne, favoured by Iraqi men. Paraffin stoves, mess tins, cooking utensils, and blue packets of Sumer cigarettes lay strewn on tables, together with a gear-box manual, in English, on the T55 tank. There was also the sign of a hasty departure. Officers' pips ripped from tunics lay scattered on the floor. Our escort was unwilling to let us venture far into the maze of underground bunkers, for the dangers of booby-traps were everywhere. He had insisted on opening any doors, using an elaborate high-kick technique. We gave a particularly wide berth to munitions invitingly left all over the ground. There were scores of damaged or destroyed vehicles, old buses, a jeep with the key still in the ignition. But these were deceptive. Much of the equipment was useless and old. Engines long since abandoned after being cannibalised for spares. The wind drove a line of cheap plastic helmets across our path. A T55, still smoking, had been caught as it backed out of its hidey-hole. The shell that smacked into its side had flipped the turret off like a lid. It was a blackened hulk. Inside death must have been instant. From another smoking ruin the sign of escape, its back doors flung open and the crew man managed to get away, dropping a lunch box of fresh tomatoes which somehow survived the inferno.

Increasingly concerned about marauding Iraqis our minders took us back to Regimental Headquarters. The place was eerily silent and it soon became clear that everyone, from Colonel Johnstone downwards, was sleeping. Some lay huddled in their uniforms, drawing warmth from their vehicles, while others had burrowed into sleeping bags. But none had removed their boots. Mike and I wanted to see the Colonel's right hand man, Major Kurt Gilles, the second in command, who we learned had taken a rather grand surrender. Major Gilles was in charge of "Step Up" a sort of parallel headquarters, so he could take control if anything happened to Johnstone's, and it was naturally some distance away. When we got there he was spooning up a breakfast of baked beans and baconburger between polishing a beautiful pearl-handled Beretta pistol. The pistol had been given to him by a captured Iraqi colonel. Kurt had literally bumped into the colonel and a handful of brigade officers. Their encounter was like something out of a romantic Hollywood costume drama. As Kurt approached the colonel stepped forward out of the darkness, snapped his heels, saluted, and said "I have your invitation." Stunned, the Major replied "What invitation? We didn't send any." To which the Iraqi, while presenting the pistol with one hand, butt first naturally, proferred a sheet of white paper. Then the penny dropped. The man was holding one of the notes dropped in their tens of thousands by American planes. As he recounted the story, over mugs of steaming tea, a salvo of rockets roared overhead heading, it seemed, in the direction of B. Company. "Oh yes, they found some Iraqis who apparently hadn't surrendered," Kurt said breezily. Amid a flurry of apologies we raced off, catching a lift on a passing lorry that was on its way to collect more prisoners.

An enemy platoon had incredibly been spotted moving around two large bunkers, right there in the middle of B company's position. Meanwhile an American artillery battery had complained that it was receiving enemy fire, and this solitary Iraqi position, clearly unaware that it was surrounded, was responsible. Because of the tiredness of his men, Potter ordered his forward observation officer,

Captain Gordon Swanston, known as the Foo, to fire an air burst over the position to force the surrender. Immediately the Iraqis, agreeably surprised, began appearing with their hands up. There were 27 of them. I had seen the power of artillery but now I understood what it must be like to be on the receiving end. Five Iraqis had been injured, one seriously. But once again all those men owed their lives to the skills of Corporal Meechan who administered morphine and saline drips, stabilised fractures and bandaged wounds. One man alone required 16 individual field dressings to stem his massive haemorrhaging. A helicopter arrived to pick up another Iraqi too badly injured to travel by lorry. When I asked one Iraqi why they had not given up earlier the prisoner said they had been told to fire their guns by their officer. So it seemed a kind of natural justice that the only man to die in the attack had been that officer, a Major who was lying beneath a sheet of corrugated plastic. The effect of the air burst had been beyond expectation. It had punched through the tops of the Iraqi armoured vehicles and made mincemeat of the flimsy shelters in which the Major and his men had concealed themselves. Yet the officer had been fatally struck by one single piece of shrapnel, the size of a steel ball-bearing which had drilled into his heart. Lt. Rob Dickson, the commander of 4 Platoon, brought the body out, and we buried him where he died, in his uniform, with his gun broken at his head, facing the direction of Mecca. It was perhaps, the most moving moment I had experienced in the desert.

Sweeping through the position Lt. Dickson discovered an arms cache and five British built Land Rovers which were later destroyed. Dickson was singled out for initiative as was Captain Swanston, of whom Potter wrote: "His timely and accurate fire mission undoubtedly saved many allied lives." In all, the action on 'Tungsten' had seen the destruction of five tanks, nine APCs, eight artillery guns, seven wheeled vehicles, and two fuel tankers.

The war was proceeding at such a phenomenal pace that orders were outstripping the plans. If it confused the Allies it left the Iraqis in chaos. They had been astonished by the speed of the advance. During an 'O' group at 1.30 pm, I could detect a new sensation. The men were relaxing, perhaps convinced that this war could not last much longer. The battle group was to move forward into a blocking position further north. As the officers studied their charts, I spotted a group of newly arrived Iraqi POWs. They had simply walked up unannounced. I spoke to one who said they had been walking for 2 days, trying to give themselves up. He was 27 and said his name was Makadid. He was pleased to be in British hands and he wanted to tell me how much he hated Saddam. I asked him about chemicals and he showed me his respirator. It was a frail Yugoslavian thing. The 'use by' date on the canister had expired 8 years earlier. It was completely useless. Makadid and the 30 other prisoners sat cross-legged with their hands on their heads. They were a pitiful sight, and you began to feel sorry for those who weren't captured. They could be left in the middle of nowhere for weeks.

The battle group moved off shortly afterwards heading now for the Wadi Al Batin, where a huge raft of Saddam's army had been left, expecting an attack which never came. But at 3.10 pm. Johnstone issued an order that signalled the war really could soon be finished. The battle group was to fire only if fired upon. Then at last light, new orders brought us to a halt and instructions for Mike and my-self. We were to go at once to Brigade Headquarters, where Christopher Hammerbeck wanted to speak to the correspondents. But it was still too dangerous to make the journey in anything as vulnerable as a Land Rover. Captain Alderson volunteered to take us in his Warrior but within minutes of setting off we came to a violent halt. We had strayed into another suspected minefield and this time the mines looked considerably larger than anything we had seen before. Alex climbed out of his turret and, gingerly walking on tracks, peered at a huge rounded impression in the sand in front of us. There were more behind. We could go neither forward or back. He decided to call an air strike by A10s to literally bomb a safe passage through the minefield for us, but the light was fading too fast and the planes were grounded. Now our safety depended on the engineers. Eventually a contraption that looked more like a com-bine harvester than a machine of war — it had a great threshing device on the front — arrived. For ten minutes a sapper examined the mound — peering at it, walking around it, and even prodding it. When he walked back to us he had a grin right across his face. "Congratulations," he said, "your minefield is the home to a family of real desert rats." The humps were made by jerboas that had, if you like, dug their own kind of shell scrapes in the sand.

The Brigadier, when we arrived, was in up-beat mood, and statis-tics of two days of action tripped off his tongue like machine gun

fire. Two Major Generals caught — six Brigadiers and "I lost count
of the Colonels." Altogether 4th Brigade had taken over 5000 prisoners and routed two mechanised Brigades, one infantry division,
one divisional headquarters, one artillery regiment, and a logistics
unit. Although the tempo the Brigade created in its night attacks
played a large part in putting the Iraqis to flight, the technology was
the key. An Iraqi battery commander taken prisoner, had told the
Brigadier how a week ago he had 100 guns and 200 men. Every day
the salvos of MLRS which proceeded the ground assault, had taken
out his guns, kilometre by square kilometre. He was left with three
guns and seven men. I reminded Hammerbeck how he had told me
back in January that the war could take until Easter to win. He
answered with candour "In my heart of hearts I thought the Iraqi
soldier would give up, but convinced myself that he would fight
hard. Those after all, were the indications we had had. It was right to
be cautious but it is astonishing how quickly we have gained the
moral ascendancy." He sounded in fact, like a man who was already
confident of victory. It was, he assured us, only a matter of hours.
He reminded me that the mission had not been about taking ground
but the destruction of Saddam's armoury, although it may be remembered as an air war he wanted to point out that a "heck of a lot
of kit had to be attended to." It was,he said a combination of air,
artillery, and the real speed of the manoeuvre battle which had
brought the imminent victory. Battle almost seemed too loose a
description, for that implies two sides fighting. This has been a one
sided affair — a walkover.

We were sitting in the mobile plans room, and all around the
Brigade staff, or Nobs, had stacked their trophies. AK47s by the
crateful; pistols, helmets, and maps which had the Iraqi positions in
blue and the Allies, (the enemy) in red. Hammerbeck had retrieved
a tank commander's uniform which he had given to the driver of his
Challenger. If the euphoria seemed faintly unseemly to me it was
only because minutes before joining the Brigadier we had heard that
a number of Fusiliers had been killed in a tragic accidental shooting.
Outside I bumped into Paul Davies, the ITN reporter who had been
travelling with the Fusiliers, and had virtually a first hand account of
what happened. He was certain that the nine soldiers who died had
been killed by Maverick missiles fired by American A10's at two
Warriors waiting to engage in enemy position. Officially the Army

were still saying the Warriors could have been struck by enemy rockets or even run over mines. Paul's version was soon proved to be utterly correct. He said there had been a sharp explosion, and one APC was engulfed in black smoke. The blast ripped a hole in the side of the vehicle, killing everyone inside, and when a second call sign went to its rescue, it too was hit. The death toll could have been far higher. The commander of the first vehicle was propelled by the explosion out of his turret and survived while several infantrymen, running to help, were blown off their feet backwards, and away from danger by the second explosion. Eleven had been maimed. It was a chastened Hammerbeck who stood beside me at 11 pm. looking at a brilliant starlit sky. He shook his head "I had hoped upon hope to bring back everyone of my soldiers."

With the arrival of Robert Fox more pressing problems came to the fore. We were both concerned that our copy was not getting through. Both Captain Irvine and Robert's minder, Captain Scoular, were hovering in the background, and to his great credit Irvine came forward offering to take our efforts now. It may have been because he was still holding a piece I had written about our visit round the battlefield and given to him almost 12 hours earlier. My despair was not lost on the Brigadier, who summoned "one of my bright young men" to make the hazardous trip, bypassing Gouldstone direct to the FTU. Mildly amusing, but prone to boastfulness, Captain Giles Gittings, was in the space of 24 hours to go from hero to villain. By the time Captain Alderson had negotiated our way back to the Royal Scots formation, it was almost midnight. The company had thrust cylumes into the sand to mark mines and the luminous glow was the only light visible. We stumbled over unfamiliar bodies around the Warrior's doors. The radio watch had been drawn from other sections to give Major Potter's crew a breather. They had dug scrapes in the sand, and Mike and I grabbed shovels from the Warrior to dig ours. But first, on hands and knees, we felt the ground we intended to excavate, gently caressing the surface for any suspicious bumps. After six weeks our desert craft was really coming on. Had we not been so tired we would probably have searched more thoroughly before abandoning caution and digging into the sand. Not for the first time spooning out the sand felt like digging a shallow grave, but it was going to mean our first lying down sleep for three days and neither of us cared too much about superstition.

# WAR

I wrote this article for the Daily Mail, Feb 27th.

Barefoot and frightened, he huddled on the ground clutching his pathetic belongings in a dirty scarf. The flash of gunfire threw his face into grotesque relief.It was the face of a defeated man. By breakfast time yesterday there were over 100 prisoners, more than one for each of B Company's magnificent fighting men. I was the only British newspaper reporter to join them as they and their battle group with tanks swept into Iraq, the pride of the Desert Rats, rolling up enemy position after enemy position. It brought moments of sheer exhilaration and sheer terror. And, at the same time, pity for Saddam's inadequate army.Such was the speed of our progress, Iraqi positions were simply over-run. They had no answer for the speed and quality of a professional fighting army.For those who did throw down their guns there was almost a sense of relief. They were the lucky ones. They would be fed, clothed but most of all they would be safe. When you saw the squalid little shell scrapes in which they had hoped to survive aerial bombardment, artillery, and to repulse the best fighting infantry in the British Army, it was a wonder they did live.

For the Scottish soldiers though, who spearheaded the British advance, it was a moment to savour. To battle honours won at Tangier, Gaza and the Somme, they can now write another chapter in their distinguished regimental history.

After an advance lasting 24 hours, B Company commander Major John Potter, his face lined with fatigue and grime, finally allowed it to crease into a smile.We had been shot at, come within inches of being blown up by mines and booby traps, but had left Iraq's border defences in disarray. Now Potter is sleeping inside the turret of his vehicle, his first rest for 36 hours.It is a sleep he will cherish. For our push has taken us miles into Iraq, further than we had dared hope, and without a single casualty. And it is a sleep he deserves. For when dusk falls tonight we shall be on the move again, engaging our next target where, this time, the enemy may be less willing to surrender.

Our journey had begun more than two days earlier when Operation Desert Sabre was launched on three fronts to liberate Kuwait. But while the Americans and French were pushing forward on their attacks, the soldiers of the British 1st Armoured Division were quietly moved up towards the border. Surprise and speed were to be our element of attack. But nothing could have prepared the generals and commanders for the progress we were to make. As details of the operation trickled over the radio we could only sit and listen, awaiting our battle signal.

It was a terrible day to go to war. Rain swept over the encampment and the winds drowned out the sound of the F16s and A10 tank killers patrolling the skies for us.By 8am Monday, as Colonel Iain Johnstone handed out his last orders, raising his voice to compete with the wind, we had changed into chemical protection suits. Passing through the border where huge breeches had been blown in the huge sand obstacles, we would be at our most vulnerable.

We set off at 1.30pm. By 4pm, just short of the border, there was an Allied war grave, marked with a white cross, the dead soldier's boots and a sheet of chemical agent repellant material.At 4.42pm we crossed into Iraq. It is a euphoric moment and also a sobering one. In a smoking pile of twisted steel was the shattered remains of an Iraqi artillery emplacement. Beside it the dismembered remains of a dead soldier.Now tracer and rocket fire was stitching a pattern across the sky. This, I thought, was definitely it. Over the radio a message scrambled in the jargon of army code warns Major Potter of Quebec Bravo Oscar — quick battle orders for an enemy position to be taken out. Now excitement and fear courses through every man but it is to be eight hours before we reach contact, finally encountering an Iraqi position that has not completely been abandoned. For hours we crawled behind A Squadron's 14 tanks. Suddenly the radio again crackles into life; we have strayed into a suspected minefield. Rockets streak over our heads. There is nothing to do but go on.

Now the tanks have a sniff of the target. Their commander, Major James Hewitt, orders them to open fire and the crump of their 120mm shells hitting dug in trenches reverberates through our reinforced vehicle. Bright illuminated rounds light up the sky and suddenly the ground is alive. Each blast sends up a fountain of sand and dirt.

Now we are outside and red and white tracer rips through the sky like a swarm of angry hornets. Then, just as it started, the snarling tanks are still and, like a mirage, appear the prisoners. One, two, a third, six marching in step with their hands on their heads. It has been a rout. We have 28 prisoners and they are lying spread — eagled at our feet. Their clothing, for it does not resemble a uniform, is tattered and worn. Their faces are frozen in terror.

Now comes the difficult bit. Several US soldiers have already died, victims of POW suicide bombers. Each man must be checked to see if he is holding a grenade, claymore or worse. Literally inches from us, Major Potter recoils. 'Mine, mine,' he screams. At fingertip reach of one of the prisoners is an anti personnel device. The POW is just as scared. He didn't even know it was there.

At first light there was another firefight. When it was over we could see smoking vehicles and the dead sprawled in the extravagant posture of men killed suddenly in battle. The survivors wanted to give up. Two surrendered to my colleague Mike Moore as he photographed the carnage. One of the men had enough poise to throw himself at our feet. 'Please. Please. Me Christian, love Jesus, don't kill.' He said his name was Sayeed and he pressed a white scarf into John Potter's hand. Then he tried to embrace Potter. It was almost the last thing he did. Slamming back the breech of his SA80, Potter said: 'Christ, I almost killed him and he only wanted to kiss me.'

There was a rattle on the side of the Warrior. It sounded like raindrops on a tin hat. In fact it was Iraqis forlornly aiming small arms fire at us. It summed up the hopelessness of their position.

A padre had come forward to give two dead Iraqis a proper burial. There was another line of prisoners. They wore flip flops or were shoeless altogether. One was forced to part with a grubby satchel. It contained his rations: three stale rolls and a packet of dates. On such sustenance Saddam must surely condemn his men.

So far it has been easy and morale is sky high. But the Desert Rats, fresh from their first victory, have a daunting task ahead: the Republican Guard.

*Feb 28.* It seemed I had barely nodded off when I was being roughly woken. It was 4.45 am. and the General was trying to shake the pair of us from our slumbers. In the end he had given us both a mighty push. Potter had already been up two hours to attend an 'O' group. Such had been the speed of our advance that the battlegroup and the Brigade had run out of maps. The charts which arrived in the early hours were of Kuwait City. Among everyone there was the sense that this meant finally fulfilling the primary objective — the liberation of Kuwait. I tuned into the 5 am. World Service news and from Washington there was talk of an imminent cease fire. At first light though, we were off at an extraordinary speed — our destination 80 kilometres away — cutting diagonally east across the Kuwaiti desert to block the road and railway north of Kuwait City, the Iraqis last freedom route to Basra. The convoy of Warriors was moving at such speed that Iraqis appearing out of the dawn mist trying to surrender, were simply bypassed — "don't stop, just point them south in the direction of Saudi Arabia, there is no time to lose." The voice of Colonel Johnstone had lost none of its clipped authority. Hundreds of Iraqis stood bemused, with their hands up, as Potter, Soutar and other commanders simply signalled with outstretched arms, to keep walking. This they could never have expected. When we crossed the Wadi into Kuwait, Mike and I erupted into cheers. Now the speed seemed to increase. It was like racing against the clock — the ceasefire must surely come at any moment but the headlong dash was to get as far as possible and as close to the fleeing Iraqis as we could before it did. Now Potter ordered gun turrets to swivel north and ordered Corporal Thompson to open the rear doors. We passed through acres of abandoned and destroyed Iraqi equipment. It was almost a blur as the tracks kicked up a curtain of sand that frequently blew back inside the Warrior. There was one grisly sight — a blackened tank with the horrible skeletal remains of the commander, burned to death, still inside the turret. Bodies were strewn across the desert floor. Their turn for burial would have to wait.

For almost two hours the advance continued, bouncing through soft and harder sand, but the urgency had somehow lessened and Potter wanted breakfast. Ben Gilchrist and I slopped water into the BeeVee and dropped in 7 MREs. Mealtimes had long ceased to have much relevance and breakfast was just as likely to be chicken stew or reconstituted omelette. We were clock-watching now and at 8 am, I snapped on the radio for the World Service headlines. This time the news was unequivocal. The US had declared a ceasefire from midnight Eastern Standard Time — exactly 8 o'clock in the desert. But within minutes the razor sharp Colonel Johnstone was on the battlegroup radio waves. "I have heard the reports of ceasefire, but until higher authorities say otherwise the operation continues," he said loftily. But on the stroke of 10 the Colonel called on 'O' group instructing officers to converge on his tactical headquarters. It was a strange mixture of mild euphoria and bewilderment, but the Colonel issued the order with a caution: "Be aware, there might well be some mad Iraqis around." If this was victory then most of us were finding it awkward to taste, backslapping was non-existent, and even handshakes were conducted with a faint embarrassment. Victory had come so quickly, so absolutely, and so suddenly it had sneaked right up on us, like someone surprising you when they touch you on the shoulder. In a way the uneasiness manifested itself in a kind of wait a minute chaps — how can it be all over? We've only just started, sensation. Certainly there was a lack of elation, not least because most officers felt that for the last two days they had been fighting an enemy that had neither the stomach nor the will for battle.

The Colonel, with an appreciation for the moment, asked Mike Moore to record victory on film. Hewitt, Potter, Soutar, Gilles, the Padre and the rest, gathered around Johnstone's warrior. It was an officers only affair, and I wandered across to a group of NCOs who were watching the episode with sad disapproval. "What about a picture of us?" they moaned. A complaint that actually did not bear much investigation. There could have been few men among 4th Brigade, let alone the Royal Scots, who had not been photographed at some stage by Mike during our association. The Colonel did not have much to say "I don't know what is going to happen next — I just want to say 'well done' to the Jocks. They have done a lot of hard training, they have done all that we asked them to do. The fact that not all of them got to clear trenches may be a disappointment. But they shouldn't be, because at least they have got out alive. We have not had a single casualty — no blue on blue. I find that very satisfying."

For an hour the talk was of the fighting that might have been — the routing of the Republican Guard — but mostly of the chemical attacks that never came. We knew they had the stuff all right, and some of the Iraqi prisoners had protective equipment, albeit flimsy, against it, but none had been used. John Potter had a theory that the Allies had from the outset a twin strategy to defeat the chemical menace. First the systematic destruction of the manufacturing capability by the SAS and the rockets that would be used to launch it, coupled with a clear and dire warning that the allies would reply in kind. Not chemicals, but nuclear assault. He was certain that at that last face to face between Tariq Aziz and James Baker back in January, the Americans made that position unquestionably plain. It was a compelling argument.

Of course the fighting had not been all one sided. The US 24th Mechanised we knew, had roared into Nasiriyah, where it fought a fierce engagement with Iraqi commandos,before shooting up the few of Saddam's war planes that had escaped bombings on airport runways. Along Highway 8 on the approach to Basra they had encountered the Hammurabi division of the Republican Guard, desperately fleeing with their tanks on the back of transporters. It was like a fairground shoot as the T72s were blown to smithereens. The Hammurabi, part of Saddam's feared elite, were flattened by artillery and rockets until broken, and they fled on foot into the darkness.

Mike Moore meanwhile, had taken James Hewitt off to photograph him standing victorious on the turret of a still smoking T55. It reminded me that we, at least, still had much to do. Somehow we had to get to Kuwait City. Sure we had always had it in the back of minds to go, but we had never thought about the practicalities. Apart from soldiers we hadn't seen a living soul who might sell us their old Chevrolet, and a street map, let alone a taxi service. I was though, anxious to move and as quickly as possible. From the World Service at least, it was not clear if correspondents had reached the city or not. The challenge of being first in was a tremendous stimulant. When I casually mentioned it to Johnstone I was expecting little more than a murmur of sympathy and the promise to "have you there in a few days." Instead his eyes lit up "What a splendid idea," he said. "Of course you must get there." With that he strode over to his adjutant, Captain Lowder in a communications vehicle and ordered "Get Captain Irvine here immediately." Our minder arrived breathless half an hour later. "I think you should take Mike and Richard to Kuwait," the Colonel said evenly. I think it was to everyone's surprise that Irvine, who had been in mid-salute as the Colonel spoke, simply answered in the affirmative. "Of course sir," he said, and that was almost that. It was decided that we should first be taken to see Brigadier Hammerbeck for his approval, and Irvine excused himself to refuel his Land Rover.

There followed a frantic hour, as Mike and I, galvanised into activity, began to throw our possessions out of Potter's Warrior and into some sort of order. Food and sweets I found at the bottom of my rucksack were handed over to Potter's crew, while a whole tinned Fortnum and Mason partridge I had been saving for just such a day I ceremonially presented to Colonel Johnstone. Two miniatures of 'Famous Grouse' scotch I had been sent for my birthday and which had been wrapped up in a pair of underpants, we quickly consumed. I had been reluctant to drink them at the time out of a curious sense of loyalty — it seemed unfair that I should have alcohol however little, while everyone else had none. Now we eked it out, one sip each, between ourselves, Potter, Johnstone, and Kurt Gilles. The Colonel had torn from a wall a chart showing our position about 40 miles north east of Kuwait City, and had given Captain Irvine a brief but essential crash course in desert navigation. There was thankfully, little time for farewells, but we posed for photographs with Potter's crew, Mike and I each rather too enthusiastically holding our captured Kalashnikovs. Our own presents from the desert which we decided to leave with Potter in the end. At Brigade Headquarters Hammerbeck was in irrepressible form, gladly posing beside a tank with his captured AK47 and a grin from ear to ear. Success had exceeded his wildest expectations. "What had won this battle was our ability to move long distances at night, with great precision in all weathers, and to attack violently from unexpected directions," he said. One Iraqi battle group had literally been caught napping. "They were in their bunkers asleep with the exception of the guards who had put up only unlimited resistance." They had never expected the night time assaults which had been the feature of the British action. The Americans, on the other hand, chose not to fight after dark because of the increased risk of fratricide, but night fighting had been at the heart of the training schedule that the British soldiers had been through in the long weeks leading up to the war. I asked him if he felt glory at the victory "No, not glory," he said reflectively, "but one does feel pride at having taken part. That above all things." He was in an expansive mood and talked on: "I have a sadness for the Iraqi soldiers — they didn't want to fight, and I am desperately sad about the Fusiliers, but I have a tremendous sense of achievement that we have made it possible for an innocent peace-loving nation to get on and do its own thing, while the perpetrators of this war are going to have to pay." These were lofty sentiments indeed, and already I wondered cynically to myself, not when, but if the Iraqis would ever pay. After all, as long as Saddam was still there then it seemed part of the brief had not been fulfilled.

Again to my surprise, Hammerbeck too readily endorsed our expedition but was cautious too. It must be a military exercise, he said. It is decided that Robert Fox and myself should travel with Irvine and Page, while Mike will ride with Captain Gittings, whose driver has a tripod mounted machine gun. We are to observe strict military discipline because of the likelihood of running into pockets of Iraqis. So we set off with Gittings leading in his vehicle, draped with so much camouflage netting that it looked more like a carnival float than a Land Rover, and a gap of around 400 yards between us.

As we set off we all feel an extraordinary sense of excitement. The tanks and trucks of the British are soon left behind and we drive into a landscape of eerie emptiness and silence. Suddenly Page brakes violently. Ahead Gittings has leaped from his vehicle and is warily approaching a shape I can barely distinguish. We slowly move closer and the shapes of two Iraqi armoured personnel carriers come into view. They contain British-made Milan anti-tank missiles, a firing post, and a heavy Browning machine gun. They have also clearly, only just been abandoned. Personal belongings are strewn in the sand away to the northeast.

It is only 4 hours since the cease fire. Between us we have 3 SA80 rifles, an ancient SLR, a machine gun and a few grenades. The equipment in front of us could have destroyed us while we were only a dot on the horizon. Now Giles is all for sticking a couple of grenades into the two vehicles. Irvine though, rightly argues that there is no knowing what the rockets might do. While at the same time the explosion would alert any scavenging Iraqis to our presence. Captain Gittings demurs and instead decides to help himself to four of the missiles and the firing pin which he lashes on to his Land Rover. "Cost £12,000 each," he confides as we set off again. But surely, I wonder, he can't be planning to sell them. We drive on more prudently beneath a sky of gun metal, blackening by the mile. Fox and I are compressed into the back of the Land Rover, sliding around amid the crates of water and compo, rucksacks and tents, that Irvine had stashed aboard. We halt again and this time there are sounds of greeting. Someone raps on the side of the Land Rover and we jump out of the back. Now we are in the middle of a huge camp. Friendly forces for sure, but who? It turns out to be a massive Egyptian logistics base and we are the first white faces they have seen. We are surrounded by a jostling friendly circus — they all want to shake our hand. Someone brings forward a tray of sweet black tea, another offers us oranges. It's marvellously spontaneous and gives us a taste of things to come. The weather meanwhile has turned fearsome — great black clouds are racing across the horizon. Gittings rechecks his bearings. A journey which should have taken no more than two hours is already close to four. Giles then unfurls a Union flag and within half an hour we climb a sandbank and slide down onto a metal road. We are on the tarmac highway, north of Kuwait City, and now the carnage of war is around us again.

Rain is shooting out of the sky and it is the edge of darkness. Destruction is everywhere. Burned out tanks, armoured cars , private cars, coaches, jeeps and the stench of death with it. We do not know it yet but this place was to symbolise the slaughter of Saddam's army. Mutla Gap on the Basra road, but it is to become universally known as the Highway to Hell. Two days earlier in a last crazed rush to escape, the occupying army of Iraqi soldiers and police in Kuwait City weighted down with loot from refrigerators to bedding, surged north in stolen vehicles. The column got no further than the Mutla Ridge where a towering escarpment suddenly breaks the flatness of the desert. There must have been more than 1500 tanks, armoured cars and private vehicles, trapped in the six lane highway. From the air, the US Navy's Silver Fox squadron descended on this immovable feast. It was as the pilots called it: "A turkey shoot." it was a still-burning junk yard of desolation, forty eight hours later. The road had been scorched away by the frenzy of fire and explosion. There was no way of knowing how many had died here, but already the vultures of war, ill-disciplined troops, and Bedouins who had ventured from the desert, were picking through the carcase of destruction for trophies. It was a dizzying and unpleasant sight. Later the slaughter here, which seemed so random, was used by those who had been uneasy about the war in the first place, as evidence of a bloodthirsty campaign being fought by the Allies. In weeks to come there is even talk that allied troops had been so disgusted by the Mutla carnage they would have refused to pursue the enemy further. As it turned out, an irrelevant point — Iraq was already beaten. I certainly did not meet a soldier or airman who, as distasteful as they surely found it, recognised the action as anything other than legitimate warfare. The tanks and APCs in that convoy were seeking to escape the war zone and would have been used to reinforce the Republican Guard. US MPs direct us off the road, around the wreckage, and we drop down the hill into the outskirts of Kuwait. It is deathly quiet, vehicles abandoned in haste everywhere; bridges with their central span blown out litter the road with rubble.

As we draw nearer the city centre it becomes wetter and darker. There is no electricity so no traffic lights or street lights to mark our way. Public buildings are pock-marked with rocket and rifle fire but we know there has been virtually no fighting in the city itself — rather, it seems, as if beaten, the Iraqis had in defeat turned their guns on buildings as some kind of pathetic revenge. When we stop to check directions the unexpected happens. Women and children dash out of the darkness, waving the black, white, red and green flags of free Kuwait, cheering 'Yankee, Yankee!' When I shout back 'We're English', they yell, 'Major, Thatcher, Desert Rats, George Bush'. It is an extraordinary sensation. We are the first Britons in uniform to drive through the streets and we all feel like liberators. Now, whenever we slow, crowds of citizens come running and skipping alongside our convoy, whistling, singing, and cheering endlessly. This is probably the first time they have ventured outside the safety of their own homes for six months. They give us flags, and we lash them to the string that hold the Union Jack. "These colours don't run," says one elderly Kuwaiti, magisterially. Even the cement-grey suburbs come alive as we sedately motor through. Uncontained relief floods the faces of these people and not for the first time I feel a phoney in my uniform. The people they should have been cheering were back in the desert burying the dead.

We had decided to head for the British Embassy and in our heart of hearts, we knew we were not going to be the first. But even so I was a little taken aback by the reception that greeted us as we turned off the Corniche. There, outside the Embassy gates, was the reassuring sight of the Daily Mail satellite telephone and colleagues David Williams, Geoff Levy and Steve Back, who had all done so much to keep my spirits up with their letters and parcels. Around them a ragtag army of Fleet Street faces in their mix-and-match uniforms, scrounged from the Brits and septics. There were also some cans of real beer and real Scotch. Our reception was overwhelming but at the same time shattering. We had made this journey with the noblest of intentions — to be first — and now we had to be content with being second best, and despite the warmth of our friends and colleagues, there was no dispelling the sense of anti-climax. There were other reunions to make. David McDine, the amiable head of the MOD's press desk back in Saudi Arabia, had arrived earlier by parachute. The grandness of the gesture — he dropped in with Marines of the Special Boat Section to reclaim the Embassy — completely overshadowed by the press, who had arrived by road laughing, at the gates below. And the satellite phone meant we could call home too. I had also promised to ring Brigadier Hammerbeck's wife, Alison, Julian James's wife, Karen, and Brigitte Potter, about to present John with a new baby. "Tell him to make sure he gets home when I'm still fat," she laughed down the line from Werl, near Dortmund in Germany. There was also a surprise in store. Colonel McDine had instructed the press liaison team he had set up in the International Hotel to provide rooms for Robert, Mike and myself. Our four army colleagues meanwhile, decided to head for the airport where the SAS had established a British section.

The International was one of the few hotels to escape Iraqi retribution and it had largely been taken over by the military. The Americans had already established a media point and the British were in the process of fixing up a more modest affair. The three of us were exhausted. "How do we get rooms," I asked. "We've got the 5th floor — just go up and help yourselves," we were told. "If a room's locked just kick the door in," added a naval officer, helpfully. Room 525 looked the most inviting sight we had seen for a long time, but appearances were deceptive. There was no running water and the toilets were in a desperate state. But we had each liberated enough bottled water from the Embassy to ensure our first wash for three days. The bed was enormous, so Mike and I decided to share, reasoning that after all we had been through, what the hell. But neither of us could sleep. After an hour I got up, unrolled my sleeping bag, and settled down to a comfortable night on the floor. Across the room Robert had done exactly the same, spurning a sofa.

*Mar 1.* When we awoke I wondered aloud to Robert and Mike when we should return to the desert. Mike had stuck his Nikon out of the window at the black clouds of smoke that hung like an oily shroud over the city's northern suburbs, where fires raged incessantly. There was no debate — we all agreed that there was nothing for us to do here and we should head back as soon as possible. I decided to try and find Irvine. It was not difficult — he had scrounged some food and he was cooking it in the press room. He said Gittings was trying to get a grid for 4th Brigade because they would almost certainly have moved since we left. That seemed sensible. In the meantime he had been asked to accept a bouquet on behalf of the grateful people of Kuwait in a ceremony to mark the city's freedom. It seemed staggering. How could it be that our minder, a man whose wartime task had been to assist press coverage, could receive the gratitude of a nation on behalf of the British Army? It seemed though, that the Kuwaitis had little choice, as there were few British soldiers in the city. Captain Irvine implored us to delay returning until after this ritual. We actually had no choice, and Mike and I both thought we might find a story to occupy a morning in Kuwait. One thing we were agreed on, we should avoid our journalistic colleagues. Most were determined to set off up the Highway to Hell while others were planning ambitiously to pursue the Iraqi Army into Basra. The human stories of the brutality of Kuwait's occupation were sure to be well documented too. From my visit here two years ago I remembered the sumptuousness of the Emir's palace. Surely that could not have escaped the vituperation of the vanquished.

We were introduced to a pleasant businessman who appeared to be a member of the Kuwaiti resistance. He volunteered little about himself but offered to be our guide. He did though, tell increasingly extravagant stories about Iraqi excesses. That they had been savage occupiers was beyond doubt, but the elaborate accounts we got of random inhumanities seemed harder to sustain. Scarcely a street he drove us down did not have its own horror story. Ten year old boys executed here; woman blinded there; rape, firing squads and retribution everywhere. At a police station there was a more measured account from a Colonel in the local resistance. He showed us a strong room of Iraqi plunder, from which Irvine who had accompanied us persuaded him to part with two bayonets, and a stack of number plates. The Iraqis would only allow Kuwaitis to drive if they fitted registrations that showed Kuwait to be a province of

Baghdad. Saddam had also printed licence plates for, we were told, Bahrain, Saudi Arabia and the Emirates. "He wanted to be Emperor of Arabia," said the Colonel. I unscrewed a Kuwaiti-Iraq plate from a wrecked Cadillac.

Negotiating entry to the Palace was not so easy, but eventually we were met by a tough but not unfriendly Kuwaiti who said he had been a member of the Emir's bodyguard. Why hadn't he fled with the rest of the Royal Family, we asked? "Because I stayed to fight," he said. The Palace, he said was normally closed to visitors, but you are Desert Rats — yes? Oh yes, we agreed, and for an hour we were given a guided tour of the state rooms and private apartments where the Iraqis had demonstrated the same kind of restraint as football hooligans. If anything, the mindless destruction here was proof positive of the rottenness of Saddam's rule. Anything that could not be stolen was systematically trashed. For Mike and me it was a satisfying scoop under the noses of our colleagues, although it later prompted Colin Smith of the Observer to say archly: "Kay didn't waste much time getting back to the Royal beat." We had planned to leave films and copy for others to transmit and round up Irvine, Fox and Gittings for the trip back to the desert, but we could not find them so set about filing ourselves. Eventually Robert arrived in a foul mood saying our minders were refusing to go back. At that point Steve Back, the Mail photographer intervened, saying he had taken pictures of Irvine dancing in the street during an impromptu carnival, that followed the flower ceremony. When I found him the Captain was changing a flat tyre on the Land Rover. He was adamant that we could not go back today — that Gittings had been unable to secure a grid reference for the Brigade and that we must all remain in town another night. It was an extraordinary situation. There were the three journalists itching to get back to the Army, while our soldier escorts wanted to stay and party. It may seem odd but I knew I was missing the desert. Back at the Embassy where the press had established camp, General Sir Peter de la Billiére, had arrived with a squadron of helicopters. Among those accompanying him, was a Brigadier who John Potter had introduced us to a week or so ago. Without spelling out the details I asked him if we could be flown back to Brigade. We were told to be ready for departure at 8 the following morning. So angry were we at being let down by Gittings and Irvine we resolved to tell neither of them of our new plans.

*Mar 2.* Just before we left the International, Mike had a spectacular and public row with Captain Irvine. Both had endured sufficient of each other and for a moment I thought the soldier was going to lose control completely. Irvine, believing that we were to drive back together, had abruptly announced that it was time to go as Robert, Mike and I made coffee. Mike flew off the handle, on the lines of: "We wanted to go yesterday — now you can wait until we want you to go." Irvine countered saying that he gave the orders. That was too much for Mike, and two months of frustration spilled out. By the time we got to the Embassy and the realisation that we had alternative travel arrangements had sunk in, Irvine and Gittings knew they were staring at the possibility of disciplinary action. In my view it had been their own stupidity and selfishness that had left them in this position, and their faces as our helicopter lifted off were a picture of misery.

Our flight took us first to Kuwait airport where the gutted remains of British Airways flight No. BA419, trapped last August 2nd, was a broken testimony to the war. Nearby a newly painted sign underlined the victory "Any time Jordan," it said. Back and over the Basra road we flew, where the altitude gave a new perspective to the carnage below. At 4th Brigade Headquarters there was an officious looking reception committee as we fluttered down, and we were marched into Hammerbeck's headquarters. If this was going to be a dressing down we were having none of it. "What have you done with my officers?" the Brigadier began. "That," we said "you can ask them when they get back." It was a disappointing finale to our weeks in the desert and inevitably the finger of suspicion was levelled by Gittings and Irvine's fellow officers at us. However, when the two captains finally did return hours later they were upbraided for their cavalier behaviour and stripped of privileges. They both had their vehicles withdrawn and were placed on 12 hour 'stags'.

For us correspondents there was one grim task outstanding — to join a burial detail as they cleared up the remains of the Iraqi dead. Near to Brigade HQ a troop truck had taken a direct hit from a Maverick missile, exploding with such ferocity that the slaughter was scattered over an area 100 metres wide. There may have been 30 bodies but it was impossible to tell. Limbs and broken torsos had been deposited like seeds on the ground. The desert had thankfully

126

begun to draw its own sandy shroud over the more grisly sights. This was the reality of modern warfare — not the smart bombs and missiles that could be fired at a target time-zones away. And yet however ghastly, I felt a sense of detachment looking at those dismembered corpses. In truth, the bodies no longer resembled human beings, but looked instead like waxworks. It was difficult to feel anything but intrusive as ten engineers with spades and a JCV arrived to bury the dead. They worked without sentiment in rubber gloves and shemaghs wound around their faces to block the stench, their assignment not just to bury, but where possible to identify the dead. Clouds of flies followed as they picked up dog tags, wallets and identity bracelets. The corpses were shovelled into a mass grave, a grid of the position taken, and in time the Red Cross would be able to contact the families of those bodies identified to tell them where their loved ones lay. Our presence seemed to have brought out a morbid curiosity. Troops who had clearly taken no part in the fighting arrived to watch. I am not sure who were the most insensitive — the soldiers who snapped away with their own cameras, or the press who did the same, but dressed it up as public interest.

The young guards officer who had been instructed to be our guide for the day, drove us on to an Iraqi logistics camp, which had been hit by a devastating air raid. B52s had stonked the place. Craters the size of quarries had obliterated buildings and vehicles. It was a dangerous expedition. Anti-personnel and cluster bombs were scattered everywhere and we all had to watch left and right as we manoeuvred across the desert. On the way we bumped into an Army air corps unit, who had just discovered a huge arms cache. Crate upon crate of AK47s and sniper rifles lay in a huge pit. The temptation was too much, and our guide, Charlie McGrath, son of the Duke of Edinburgh's private secretary, set up an impromptu shooting range. Helping ourselves to Kalashnikovs and pistols we blazed our way through several magazine clips. Nearby, I had spotted another bunker system which had not been investigated and when I broke open the door I discovered it was a vast armoury. Here there were further crates, but this time of brand new automatic rifles, and what's more, stamped 'Kingdom of Jordan' and dated. The dates were December 31, months after the embargo on sales to Iraq had been introduced and convincing evidence that the Hashemite Kingdom had provided more than succour and rhetoric for Saddam. There were Chinese manufactured AKs, with folding stocks, and Soviet ones with bayonets attached. Mike and I helped ourselves to a crate, but quite what we thought we would do with them, we didn't know.

Later at an intelligence O group, I learned that the Allies believed that Saddam had been killed on the night before the war stopped. American planes had dropped 40 precision bombs on selected targets in Baghdad, including the bunker where the Iraqi leader was thought to have been holed up 200 ft. underground. They knew there were casualties but not for the first time intelligence proved to be wanting. Already its assessment of Iraqi defences had been proved wrong. Minefields meant to be 2,000 yards deep turned out to be only 140 yards. Oil and napalm filled trenches, talked of as huge reservoirs were only a couple of yards wide. The sand berms were pathetic and underground bunkers miserable holes in the ground, lined with corrugated plastic and a few sandbags, inadequate to prevent any explosion. While the Iraqi soldiers themselves did not measure up to the menacing warriors they had been built up to be.

Just how many casualties the Allies inflicted on Iraq was unclear. Certainly the death toll had been very heavy. At the border berm thousands were thought to have perished, buried alive as the sand walls were bulldozed aside. Brigadier Hammerbeck's own assessment was that 44 Iraqi divisions had been destroyed, with 80,000 dead and 200,000 prisoners. Despite the commanders pride and satisfaction at victory, there were misgivings too. It had clearly been one of the great mis-matches of military history. Around 3,850 of Iraq's tanks had been destroyed, far more than the 2,700 Germany lost in the Battle for Kursk, regarded by historians as one of the greatest ever tank battles. If anything, the land battle could be compared to Agincourt, where for a handful of dead, English longbowmen killed 10,000 Frenchmen.

*Mar 3.* It is extraordinary, but the atmosphere has changed incontrovertibly. I have remained billeted at Brigade HQ, sleeping in a corner of Major Julian James's tent. In an instant, soldiers have switched to relaxation mode. Respirators are no longer required to be carried, and in place of helmets berets are flourishing, revealing to me for the first time the huge diversity of regiments and disciplines distinguished by different cap badges that make up a brigade. Stand to has been scaled down, and in the cookhouse they have tuned the radio away from the World Service to the pop of Desert Shield FM. I have decided to remain with the military for a few more days. Somehow I don't feel ready for a headlong dash back to civilian life, and besides, the Prime Minister is expected. Mike Moore is to remain a further 24 hours in order to record Tom King's visit to the troops. Major's date is not yet known . Fox too, waits on but our other colleagues are leaving. Paul Davis's departure had left a sour taste in Hammerbeck's mouth. When he left the ITN man had apparently spoken to the Brigadier. Now Hammerbeck was asking me if I thought this had been a *real* war. He went on: "Have we not prosecuted this war to a victory of stunning success? Wasn't that what was required?" I could only agree, but the soldier carried on "No, this was not a land war for television, there weren't enough bodies for them. No blood and guts to film. Well that's tough. Whether television likes it or not this will go down in history as one of the greatest military victories ever." It was clear that Davies and his camera man, Nigel Thompson, who used to joke about going into battle standing on the turret of a Challenger, had not got the footage that would win for the reporter a second "TV Journalist of the Year Award". Most of the British action had been confined to darkness, not conducive to good pictures, and the Fusiliers with whom they travelled, had remained at the margin of infantry action. Seventh Brigade had not fared much better. A tape of Martin Bell's showing the Staffordshires in action clearing trenches had been lost.

The days that followed were mellow and easy going with the weather swinging alarmingly between sunshine and extreme cold. At times the effect of the 600 oil wells Saddam's defeated army had set alight as a punitive petulant gesture, turned the landscape around Kuwait City into one like Dante's Inferno, and even 40 miles away it had the effect of turning the sky apocalyptic. The wind would drive acrid yellow clouds across the sky and noon on March 5th was like midnight. Mike Gouldstone described it as Golgothic — like he said, the colour the sky turned to at Christ's crucifixion.

After the miserably cold weather of the past weeks, the day time temperature has soared — high enough for soldiers now on a relaxed schedule to strip to the waist for boisterous games of volleyball. But there are some honourable exceptions. There are no bare-chested Royal Scots and unlike the rest of the Brigade who have dispensed with respirator and helmet, Colonel Johnstone has kept his men at battle readiness. This is not out of any sense of pique but rather one of discipline. The death of Tom Haggerty, killed when he stepped on a mine as he adjusted the slack on the track of his Warrior, was a tragic reminder of the dangers still lurking in the sand. A flak jacket may not have saved Haggerty but they were still a safety cushion against blasts.

Nothing, no flak jacket nor armour plating could have saved the lives of the nine British servicemen who were the victims of American friendly fire — a gross phrase that does not do justice to the crime. Although I had not spent much time with the Fusiliers a message reached me that the commander of C company, Major Alec Bain and soldiers from 8 platoon, who were implicitly involved, wanted to talk about the tragedy. They were on a roller coaster of emotions switching from grief to anger. Their reconstruction as we sat cross-legged in the damp sand was still, five days after the event, one of incomprehension.

Corporal Phillip Forsyth shook his head. "It was such a waste," he said. "If we had been jumping into trenches to meet the enemy face to face, at the end of bayonets and the lads had been killed that way, that would have been them doing their job. But to be sitting in the back of a wagon doing absolutely nothing, not knowing what was going on, and to be hit by friendly aircraft...it makes it worse."

What they first told me came as a surprise. Far from the poor weather conditions that we were told had contributed to the error, the sky was blue and virtually cloudless. "It was one of those days in the desert when you can spot anything for miles," one soldier said. Like the other battlegroups, the 3rd battalion, the Royal Regiment of Fusiliers had been slicing through Iraqi positions so rapidly the operation had become a pursuit. But unlike the Royal Scots there had been fewer engagements with the enemy.

As part of the brigade attack on objective codenamed Brass, C company were to attack a horseshoe-shaped Iraqi gun emplacement containing dug-in D20 and D30 artillery pieces. It had already been hammered from the air by B-52s but the Warriors still poured heavy cannon fire on to the position. Then the barrage stopped and Major Bain ordered sappers to finish the task by wiring up any serviceable equipment and exploding it. It was then around 3pm and under the bright sky, the Warrior crews of 8 platoon relaxed. Some stretched their legs, others brewed tea.

"The sappers were to give us warnings before each explosion and I was rotating my turret to check that people were out of harm's way," explained Major Bain. "Suddenly there was one particular bang which I thought was a bit quick and through my sights I saw 22 brewing up. At first I thought the sappers had made a terrible mistake, that they were somehow responsible. Then when I saw a man running to help drop to the ground I had only one thought — mines. Callsign 23 was already coming alongside to help when it too went up. I was convinced we were in a minefield and I ordered the company to stay back while I advanced backwards to about 100 metres. Ahead of me a soldier I couldn't recognise was face down in the sand dragging another man. They were both hurt and had made about ten to 15 metres when someone dashed from behind to help. Some people were on top of 22 now, trying to reach those who had been trapped inside. My gunner swore he could see someone moving beneath the flames but there couldn't have been anyone in there alive."

Major Bain and his men now feared the two Warriors had been struck by rounds fired from a shoulder-held RPG team. Amid all the shock he adopted the most sensible course, ordering the company back into the advance. "I knew that we would have to go on, but first I would have to identify the dead. Twice before I have seen death on such a scale in Ireland but a high explosive missile does terrible things to a human being. Just to keep up my morale I had to get someone to come with me. I called the padre up too and got the sappers to cover the dead with sheets of CARM."

Despite the horror there were heroic displays of professionalism by the medics who saved at least one life by performing an immediate tracheotomy on a Corporal Fyfe before helicopters could arrive to transfer the survivors to a field hospital. "The bravery I saw that day was automatic, it was based on friendship and trust. It is one of the reasons why we go to war in small units. It makes you want to do something for someone else because you trust he will do something for you. Two of my soldiers ran into that nightmare to try to save their friends and in both cases they failed, one lost his life doing so. We will never forget that."

Eight platoon's sergeant, who saw two thirds of his men killed or injured, said "The only way to describe such a loss is that you are in a family of 35 and nine of them get taken away from you. You feel as if you have lost nine of your sons."

Within minutes the full implication of the attack began to sink in. It had been neither mines nor RPGs but Maverick missiles fired from the sky by a pair of patrolling American A 10 tankbusters. How and why this tragedy happened would never properly be explained. Had the US pilots failed to distinguish between British Warrior combat vehicles and the Iraqi equivalent, the Soviet-made BMP1 or BMP2? It seems highly unlikely, the two vehicles are very different with the Warrior having a much higher profile off the ground. In addition, and crucially, the Warriors — like all coalition vehicles carried three special markings. An inverted black V (the Arab figure 8), a fluorescent vest attached to the turret and a red warning light fixed to a stalk at the back. Above all, many of the British vehicles carried the Union Jack too. Where there could be room for doubt, and I stress the word could, is that many of the Fusiliers' Warriors had cladding wrapped around their Rarden cannons exaggerating the size of the barrel. Is it possible that this distorted the shape to the two pilots two miles up in the sky? No, I think what is likely is that the American planes were simply in the wrong sector and were anyway too far away when they fired their missiles to know what their target was. It remained the saddest and sourest episode of the war and, to the relatives of those who died and were maimed, unsatisfactorily resolved. It is not enough to say that accidents happen in wartime, the families deserve the fullest of apologies from both the Americans and the Ministry of Defence together with appropriate compensation.

Back at headquarters the graveyard of abandoned or damaged Iraqi vehicles being assembled by the Royal Engineers was assuming the proportions of a used car lot. A score of T55s and countless anti-aircraft pieces like SA 13s have been towed, dragged and even driven into a bulldozed acre just behind brigade headquarters. To my inexperienced eye much of it seems rusted and obsolete but there again, perhaps worthy of the inadequate army to whom it was entrusted. Brigadier Hammerbeck, who has learned from a signal that the Prime Minister will visit the brigade, is very proud of the collection and intends showing it off to Mr Major. There is another more pressing reason to gather in all enemy equipment because of fears of booby traps. Some Iraqis cannot have been in such a hurry to run as the Allies advanced because they found time to leave behind crude but effective booby traps. These included fixing hand-grenades to the turrets of tanks with wire looped through the pin so they detonate on opening the lid. General de la Billiére, had averted a near certain tragedy himself when he spotted a device dangling from an Iraqi machine gun. The potentially lethal contraption had been loaded into his helicopter by one of his pilots.

In the late afternoon sun Mike and I together with Captain Scoular as minder leave for divisional headquarters where the Defence Secretary Tom King is expected in the morning. This time, because our navigator knows how to navigate, our journey is a fraction of the hours we took last week on the same trip. The carnage on the Basra road remains a grisly sight. Although most of the bodies are said to have been removed, clouds of flies tell a different story. The real parasites though are the Arabs who have driven up from their newly-liberated city to loot, scavenge and plunder from the corpses and tangled wreckage. A few soldiers, pose for pictures beside the burned out hulks and even Mike and I cannot resist standing beside a still-smouldering T 62 tank in matching khaki tee shirts emblazoned with the words 'Law 80 — the best bang this side of Baghdad'. The anti-tank weapon had actually had mixed results in the war but the picture would have been a marketing man's dream.

General Smith had established his headquarters in shade half an hour's drive north of Kuwait City. Before the Iraqi invasion it had been proposed as a site for a holiday camp but it can never have been a fragrant spot. It had an odour of dank sewage and decay — and it was a breeding ground for mosquitos. Captured anti-aircraft guns and a dead tank stood sentinel at the entrance. Olive and khaki tents had mushroomed everywhere, including one for the correspondents who had been based at Division. They had certainly enjoyed a more comfortable war: a tent, sufficient water, cookhouse food, even electric light. Inside, the press tent was arranged like hospital ward, about a dozen neat camp beds and a handful of canvas chairs. Kate Adie was the redoubtable and formidable figurehead of the group. She was of course the forces' number one pin-up, but at home I knew from letters, Kate had been criticised for some of her livelier, at-the-front style reporting. We'd all been amused after one singular despatch was described to us when she had apparently appeared on screen all buttoned up in a flak jacket — and earrings. However, I was a great admirer of Kate's. Not only had she overcome Army top brass reluctance to let a woman cover a war from the sharp-end, she'd also had to withstand personal privations which the rest of us could only guess at. Her hazards were not just the anti-personnel mines we routinely had to avoid but also the intrusive eyes of soldiers who had not seen a woman for months. "When you've managed to wash and go to the loo with a measure of dignity out here avoiding the peeping toms you do feel rather satisfied," she told me with typical understatement. At no time could she relax in privacy having to share a tent with the other male correspondents. I'm sure her composure played no small part in General Smith's very appropriate decision to award her a medal all of her own — a beautiful silver replica of a long-tailed desert rat.

For the first time I was actually at the end of the line to observe what has been happening to my copy once I've finished it. My last piece to be submitted to the censors was about the burial detail we'd joined a couple of days ago. Surprisingly, because it was a deliberately uncomfortable report there were no deletions on the grounds of taste, just a minor one on accuracy. It was the task of Colonels King and Sexton to review stories, removing anything which might be useful to the enemy — positions, strengths and supplies, for example — with a large black pen. As censors go they were far from zealous showing a flexibility that would never have been permitted nine years earlier during the Falklands War. But at the same time they were curiously inconsistent. Early on I had written about inoculations soldiers were lining up to receive for anthrax and other ghastly diseases to which the colonels had not objected. But when I later wrote about bubonic plague prevention it was obliterated from the page and I received a verbal ticking-off for breaching operational secrets. By now though the censors had completed their brief and when Tom King arrived on March 4th our despatches were not required to go before them.

Mr King had come to give the tonic the troops waited to hear — an early return from the desert. His arrival on a sticky morning brought another surprise in the shape of my editor, Sir David English, one of four editors invited to travel out from London. The others were Max Hastings of the Daily Telegraph, John Birt, the Director General designate of the BBC and ITN's Stewart Purvis. For myself and Robert Fox it was a warm and affectionate greeting from two highly respected newspaper editors who knew all about wars themselves — English in Vietnam and Hastings in the Falklands. They were instantly at home in the surroundings.

King's brief was not just to promise the troops the biggest welcome home party ever but also to compliment the architects of the victory, General Smith and his commanders. Smith, was awkward in the company of praise and sat twiddling his spectacles as King heaped more and more of the stuff on his slim shoulders. He told how the support at home for the war had been incredible. "I have never known anything like it," he said, "the whole emotion of it." He joked that there was a feeling the success had been won single handed by Scotland, a reference to the huge numbers of Scottish soldiers in the Army and ironic when King's own plans for the Scottish Division, soon to be unveiled, would deal a disproportionate blow north of the border. The number one priority, he said, was to secure the release of all POWs from Iraq, followed by ratification of the ceasefire — nobody really knew the status of the Iraqi generals who had signed the thing at Safwan over the weekend. It would mean soldiers remaining in the desert for, at the most, another six weeks. "The worst mistake we could make would be to let everything we have achieved, in this remarkable campaign, slip away."

In his slacks and open neck shirt King struck the exact note. There was no triumphalism, no gloating, just satisfaction at a job well done. This seemed to me wholly appropriate. It was a shame though that in the weeks to come he could not share this reasonable approach when he yielded to economic demands for cuts to the Army so soon after its magnificent achievement.

General Smith, who reminds me of a youngish Richard Burton and is perhaps the cleverest man in the Army, prefers the company of soldiers to politicians and journalists. But he tackled this non-military audience with equanimity and set the feat of the last few days in terms we could all understand. In the 100 hours of the ground campaign we had covered the equivalent distance of Cherbourg to Berlin with the actual fighting corresponding to somewhere around Munster. What was more revealing was the capability of the First Armoured Division. It had consumed 2.2 million litres of fuel in the 350 kilometres from breach to standstill but there was sufficient reserve to take the 4th and 7th Brigades all the way to Basra as had been the original plan until Bush stopped the war. That statistic alone proved the British supply chain was superior to that of its allies. Indeed the Americans who had pushed much deeper into Iraq found their own was stretched beyond its limit. The pursuit of the fleeing remnants of Republican Guard divisions stuttered as M1A1s were forced to syphon petrol from one tank to another. The case for Challenger seemed overwhelming when Christopher Hammerbeck pointed out that not only had it outgunned everything on the battlefield but also that out of his force of 59 a maximum of four was ever out of commission at any one time.

Mike Moore and I had found true friendship in these weeks in the desert. Thrown together for the most extraordinary of reasons it had been borne out of a deep respect, not circumstance. Of course there were times when each irritated the other, when a remark was made that might have caused dissent. Both of us would then hold our breath and count to ten and then find that the problem had receded into more manageable proportions. But these moments were rare, mostly we had an emotional attachment that springs, I am certain, from experience of war, however brief it may be and his departure was tinged with sadness. Of course I understood his reasons, as a father of a son he had scarcely seen — Harry was as old as the Iraqi invasion and most of that time Mike had spent in the Gulf — he was anxious to get home. There was no time for formalities as we shaved in a rain shower before I hurried off with Robert Fox to meet a helicopter which was detailed to fly us back to 4th Brigade HQ. The weather was appalling, rain and a thick sulphureous sky made visibility virtually nil and it was a wonder the Army Air Corps crew were prepared to risk their necks, let alone ours. But the Lynx eagerly nosed off into the storm.

We were to join Hammerbeck and a handful of his senior officers to spend part of the day exchanging walnut cake and coffee with Colonel David Weisman, the commander of the US Third Brigade. It was a revealing visit. The colonel told how his men had made the hideous discovery of bodies of Iraqi soldiers staked to the ground in some barbarous modern day equivalent of the firing squad for deserters. They showed evidence of being badly beaten and tortured too, apparently because they had been found carrying in their tunic pockets the Allies' leaflets on how to surrender. Intelligence indicated that death squads had been set up by fanatical officers in a ruthless attempt to force their unwilling soldiers to fight. "Had we fought them during daylight I think they would have been willing to surrender," said the Colonel. "But at night I think they were so frightened anyway they decided to put up something of a fight." He had lost eight men, he did not care to say how many Iraqis had died though. To the Colonel who had joined the US Army during the darkest days of Vietnam, there was no denying his satisfaction at victory. In the last hours of the war, he told us, an American tank squadron in hot pursuit in the Euphrates valley had trapped the remnants of the Medina Division of the Republican Guard and blasted 81 tanks, 95 APCs and 15 anti-aircraft pieces. He put it simply. "In my 24 years in the military we have the best equipment and best soldiers we have ever had." Brigadier Hammerbeck, though, pointed out that Iraqi artillery had outranged anything the coalition forces had to offer. "They just hadn't got their act together," he said. "If they had, if their officers hadn't run away and if they'd found that will to fight, the war would still be going on." The two commanders agreed that air power alone, although fundamental, would not have decided the argument. Before leaving, Weisman presented Hammerbeck with a souvenir, a deactivated Iraqi rocket. He could use it as a paperweight.

Red and blue flares were the only patch of colour as the Puma corkscrewed out of a leaden sky. Before its rotor blades had stilled, the door of the helicopter slid open and John Major was jumping into the sand. After 30 hours of continuous rain March 6th had opened to storm force winds which tore clouds of grit across the skyline. The Prime Minister, who was on his way back to London from a post-war conference with Gorbachev in Moscow and had detoured to meet the Desert Rats, pointed a colleague towards a blacker gloom on the horizon where smoke and flame were pouring from wounded oil wells. The first Allied leader to visit liberated Kuwait was determined to appreciate every bit of it.

It started quite properly with the men of the 4th Armoured Brigade whose orders to move to the Gulf were among the very first he gave from the Prime Ministerial desk at Downing Street. Christopher Hammerbeck had assembled 1,000 or so of them, drawn from the infantry, tanks, artillery and logisitical units, against the now vast junkyard of broken and captured Iraqi tanks and guns. The cook, who had found his catering interrupted when 250 Iraqis surrendered to his mess crew, had returned to more familiar duties. He handed Mr Major a steaming mug of coffee and a tray of flapjacks.

Like Tom King before him, the Prime Minister had come to salute the bravery of British troops. Instead of speeches, though, what he wanted to do was to shake as many by the hand as he could. If he had called an election the next day he would have had it in the bag. There was nothing grey about this performance as he squeezed his way through a crush of sand and khaki uniforms. Someone pushed a Chelsea FC shirt into one hand. Brigadier Hammerbeck had a more effective trophy; a captured AK-47, deactivated, of course. Grasping the rifle and an enemy helmet he joked: "This will give me Cabinet authority of a sort — just wait till we discuss public expenditure next year."

Such was the warmth that enveloped him that his message of congratulations could scarcely be heard above the din. But he did tell them: "The degree of pride and support back home in the way you have performed is more than anything you can imagine." Glancing across at Hammerbeck he grinned: "You will be amazed at how many of your commanders have become folk heroes. And in a tribute to the strategy that made it all possible he had this to say: "It was a marvellous operation, perhaps the most successful in war ever."

Mostly all he wanted to say was thank you. And he did, over and over again. Before he left for a rendezvous across the desert with 7th Brigade and then the frigate Brave, off the Kuwaiti coast, Major turned to have a brief word with Robert Fox and me, commending us for our humbler role in the affair. The quality of the reporting had been of a high standard, he volunteered.

Prime Ministers may not usually be the most sentimental of creatures but journalists, for all their ephemeral concerns, often are, so it seemed a fitting time to leave. My time in the desert had run a natural course. I also needed to return to divisional headquarters to file a despatch on Major's visit. I wanted, though, to say some farewells myself, not least to those at the Royal Scots who had become close friends.

I found Lt Col Iain Johnstone sitting in his command Land Rover in pensive mood — perhaps still thinking about where he was going to get his hands on all those windscreens. As we bumped across the furrows in the sand to the battallion's position, he presented this curious piece of advice on going home. "You may find it very strange, uncomfortable even. Don't be surprised if you want to spend a lot of time on your own." This, at any rate, was the testament of his experience of 20 years of Army life.

In the few days since hostilities ended the battalion had moved easily from trenches back to tents. Evidence of the battleground was still all around; minefields marked with razor wire, shards of twisted metal and scorched, doomed Iraqi tanks. John Potter had placed B company on a ridge, the guns of the Warriors pointing north towards Baghdad. He and Alex Alderson had established a command post with a chair, table and, of course, their treasured American cots. Still vigilant — they were the only soldiers still wearing body armour — the jocks had just caught an Iraqi soldier who had apparently been hiding in a shell scrape for days. When out of curiosity and hunger he had popped his head out of the sand it was hard to say who was the more surprised. The Scots were the more prescient, producing nothing more threatening than a camera to record the event.

After brisk goodbyes I returned to brigade HQ where there was another round of handshaking with Brigadier Hammerbeck, Mike Gouldstone and the other minders and drivers. I had one more task: to dispose of my collection of looted Iraqi guns. Taken in the heat of the moment, they had assumed the size of a small armoury. Half a dozen AK 47s, an ancient bolt action snipers rifle, holsters, webbing, ammunition clips and all in that box stamped Kingdom of Jordan. I wrapped two Kalashnikovs, one Russian and one Chinese, in a bed roll and wondered how I could get them deactivated. I need not have worried, the Army had no intention of letting any military souvenirs leave the country. After the Falklands hundreds of Argentine weapons were smuggled back to Britain, this time only those destined for regimental museums would be permitted to leave. But, as I learned the next day, regimental museums could be applied to well, almost anything. Just tell the RAF people that you are donating them all to decorate the Daily Mail boardroom, an officer had hissed in my ear.

It did not matter, the only souvenir I actually treasured was my official war correspondent accreditation. But there was a snag, the Army as capricious as ever, wanted the white warrant cards back. To avoid hurt feelings, because I was determined not to part with mine, I informed Mike Gouldstone it had been lost. He presented me with a bundle of letters — the mail which had been delayed by hostilities was now arriving with super efficiency. Among the correspondence was a letter from a Daily Mail reader and mother of a young soldier who had been at the heart of the fighting. Our despatches had made her feel closer to her son, she wrote.

Together with Robert Fox, who had elected to stay for a few more days, I was driven down to divisional headquarters for the last time. Once again our route took us down Saddams' road to ruin where the Allies had exercised a questionable right to cull. How many bodies had been bulldozed under the sand, I wondered.

Most of the FTU crew had packed their bags and gone and the rest would be leaving with me in the morning. In the communications truck I found a BBC editor putting the final touches to a very slick video which he and his colleagues were going to present to Patrick Cordingley. It looked terribly impressive: fast-tracking action set to Phil Collins' In the Air Tonight. Eye-catching it may have been but it was, in fact, footage shot of 7th Brigade's last full-scale exercise before a single shot had been fired in anger. It seemed a fitting epitaph to television's experience of the ground war.

At 8am we left in a convoy of trucks. What was left of my kit I had given away or, in the case of soiled clothing, buried in the sand. Dropping down from the Mutla Ridge into Kuwait City there was a brief stop at the Joint Information Bureau, firmly established in the International Hotel. It has become hack city crawling with journalists and TV crews in newly pressed desert combs. Definitely time to get out. Among those we picked up was Ramsay Smith, with whom I had flown to Saudi weeks earlier. He, like my colleague Dave Williams, had distinguished himself by following the Arab forces as they had advanced on Kuwait City — dangerous enough — but then filing gripping despatches from satellite phones they set up in the desert.

The RAF had agreed to fly all the accredited correspondents out of the city on a Hercules. Most carried a trophy of some sort and between us we had enough guns to start a small war. Which is just the way the RAF saw it. At the airport they asked us to hand the lot over. With a measure of relief we duly did.

An hour's flight took us to Al Jubail, across the Saudi border where I bumped into Major Norman Soutar who had just performed one of his saddest tasks, accompanying the coffin of Tom Haggerty, (the only soldier in the Royal Scots to die in the desert — two days after the ceasefire) to the port for transport home.

From the RAF base we thumbed a lift in vain until an American serviceman with a lorry load of cushions picked us up. At a hotel we pooled the few riyals we had left for a meal, which we ate off china. That night I bathed in hot water and slept in a bed between sheets. But Saudi Arabia was to pull one last trick.

I needed a day or two to acclimatize myself to civilian life again, which was just as well. After all the difficulties that were manifest in getting in to the country, I found leaving Saudi equally hard. Because I had flown in with the RAF, automatically avoiding immigration there was no entry visa in my passport. So they would not grant an exit stamp. How can we let you leave the country if you have never been here, they said helpfully? Somehow I suppose I expected Saudis to be a little more generous, a little more understanding. American and British soldiers had defended their country at some cost and driven the enemy from their door. Where the Kuwaitis were churlish, Saudis were ungrateful, ungracious and downright awkward. Patience, a virtue the Arabs possess in abundance, won the day and 24 hours later my passport was duly stamped for departure.

Three of us, Ramsay and Mirror photographer Ken Lennox, crammed into a taxi for the drive across the narrow causeway that divides Saudi from Bahrain and glasses of cold beer. The drink was made a little less palatable by our driver's final demand. For a 90 miniute trip he charged us $650.

Two days later we were bound for London and thanks to a stewardess who had watched us hungrily devour our first quarter bottle of Lanson, Ramsay and I managed to get very pleasantly drunk on the way home. I was sober enough to ensure I caught sight of the English countryside coming up below the clouds over the Isle of Wight. The fields and hedgerows were only just shaking off their winter coats, but after the grey porridge of Araby sands they looked wonderful. Two days later David English threw a lavish black-tie party for all his returning war correspondents — David Williams, Geoffrey Levy and Steve Back who had all journeyed into Kuwait, and Paul Harris who had endured an even more uncertain few weeks in Tel Aviv where Scuds had dropped out of the sky with alarming frequency.

I had hoped for a holiday, but the Daily Mail had other ideas Presumably working on the principle that you should always re-mount a horse after falling off, I found myself writing about the private life of Princess Anne's former husband Mark Phillips. Some-how it seemed I had turned full circle.

# POSTSCRIPT

Some very powerful names were invoked before, during, and after the Gulf War. Saddam vowed to make "our province of Kuwait" another Vietnam. George Bush, equally feisty, declared that, "thanks to God we've kicked the Vietnam syndrome once and for all" when Allah willed otherwise. From start to finish the 'Vietnam experience' coloured this short, sharp conflict. It was etched deep in the Arabian sands but in the aftermath of victory it projected an image that was hugely distorting.

There were, of course, some compelling comparisons. The enemy in both cases was a backward, rural dictatorship equipped with both home-made and modern weapons. America, who at the height of Vietnam had somewhere over half a million soldiers in South East Asia and a similar number in the Gulf, led in both wars alliances built on the loftiest of motives. But while Vietnam, for a host of geographic, political and moral reasons could not be won, in Iraq for all the stories of Saddam's might—his vast standing army, poison gas and biological weapons—there could only be one conclusion. Everything favoured the coalition. In aircraft and space-age technology the superiority was 4 to 1, in men (and a few women) in the battle zone 2 to 1. In population alone the Allies had a pool of 420 million to Iraq's 16 million. If all else failed, the Americans had, in offshore carrier groups, some 1,000 nuclear weapons. It was not conceivable that Saddam could win a war against such odds, let alone keep his jackbooted troops inside Kuwait.

The mercifully light casualty figures on the winning side have no parallel this century—148 Americans, 42 Britons and many of those the victims of friendly fire. (Indeed the US lost almost as many men in traffic accidents on Saudi Arabia's roads before a single shot was

143

fired in anger.) Such a pushover will inevitably lead to historical comparisons, such as Clive's victory at Plassey in 1757 when, for the loss of 22 soldiers, he destroyed an army of 60,000 Indians. But where Clive's win paved the way for the birth of an empire, victory in the Gulf routed an army but left in place the regime it was designed to topple. It should not be forgotten that, in a way, Saddam was a creature of the West, encouraged by Britain and America to pursue his aggression against Iran in the infinitely bloodier first Gulf War. British complicity in Saddam's supergun project is just one of the uneasy discoveries now overshadowing the successful prosecution of the war.

Two years on from his army's expulsion from Kuwait, Saddam remains in power in Baghdad, beaten but unbowed, arrogant and ruthless. A defiant, devious tyrant as bellicose as ever, still tempting another US strike that would aim to complete the job left unfinished on February 28th 1991. This is not to say the war in the Gulf was not worth it. A vital principle was defended: aggression will be checked—at least when the victim is custodian of the most crucial commodity in the world. But on most other fronts the euphoria of victory has given way to traditional pessimism. The new alliances which brought much credit to Bush two years ago have not lasted and the region's historic distrust of the West has barely receded.

The much vaunted promise of a new world order looks suspiciously like the old world order. The Kuwaiti royal family has been restored to power with pre-war talk of democracy remaining just talk. Saudi Arabia, whose cruel, degrading system was opened to scrutiny when its borders contained so many foreign servicemen, has shrunk back behind its veil of secrecy while Iraq remains a barbaric fiefdom.

Within weeks of that intoxicating success the polish on the victor's cup was already looking tarnished. George Bush had entreated the people of Iraq to rise up and throw Saddam and his wicked regime out. But when the uprisings by the Shia's in the marshlands of southern Iraq and the Kurds in the north east were met by brutal resistance from Saddam the Allies sat back, wrung their hands and did nothing. The boasts of March that his great army had been marginalised and rendered powerless were hollow. Displaying none of the tactical ineptitude it had against the Allies, the Iraqi army marched first south to Basra flattening the pitifully-armed resistance there and then on to Sulaymaniyah to smash the Kurdish rebellion. Had the West even armed the rebels then the insurrections might have succeeded. But like the decision to halt the headlong dash into Iraq, the non-intervention a month later displayed a flawed judgement. Then Britain had argued for hostilities to continue but the American view, that the fighting should stop, prevailed. According to Sir Charles Powell, Margaret Thatcher's foreign policy advisor, the timing of the ceasefire allowed the Iraqis to withdraw tanks and other equipment they were later to use with such devastating effect on their own people.

"My clear recollection is that the advice which the American commanders and American military leaders gave at that time was that there really were no targets left to shoot at," he said. They indicated that it was not in the tradition of the US Army to "shoot people in the back as they were running away from their tanks." The British misgivings carry some weight. According to Powell, the British did not believe "the loop had been completely closed around the Iraqi forces in and around Kuwait. We wanted to be sure that was done because we wanted to inflict the greatest possible defeat on Saddam Hussein." He added: "I think perhaps it did come as a surprise that there had been an outbreak of what I remember someone described as unaccustomed chivalry on the Western side. Perhaps with the benefit of hindsight, if we'd gone on for 12 more hours greater military damage would have been done."

Popular opinion forced John Major to take the upper hand when the plight of the Kurdish refugees on our television screens could no longer be ignored. Within weeks of the war ending British troops, this time Royal Marines, were back in Iraq policing a demilitarized zone and building camps for a displaced population of epic proportions. The dream of an independent Kurdistan simply evaporated. When I visited UN-controlled northern Iraq, the scale of the destruction and misery his troops had inflicted on the Kurdish people horrified me. Stories of torture and slaughter were rife. The sight of Kurds pouring over the mountains towards Zakho and the Turkish border bringing with them tales of genocide threw up just one question: why? Had not British and American lives been lost to prevent such brutality recurring? The answer, of course, was yes and no. The uncomfortable fact is that while there was a desire to see Saddam removed from power there was concern too at the destabilising prospect of an Iraq dividing into three much weaker individual states that would inevitably attract the ambitions of stronger neighbours, notably Iran. If that meant an Iraq which ensured the survival of the butcher of Iraq then so be it. Indeed, Bush's assurance a month into Desert Storm to the people of Iraq that it was not them but their leader with whom he was in conflict, seems now so hollow. For two years on with the country still in the grip of the world's economic blockade it is the people of Iraq who are dying of sickness and starvation, while Saddam himself survives.

Of course, attempts to emasculate the dictator continue. Under the terms of the ceasefire all of Iraq's biological and chemical weapons are to be destroyed, as are its ballistic missiles with a range exceeding 100 miles and its ability to develop a nuclear bomb. Yet when required to produce an inventory of these arms and facilities, Baghdad cheated shamelessly, underestimating its chemical stocks and claiming to possess neither biological weapons nor nuclear grade material. The work of the UN commission has been frustrated and thwarted at every turn and it remains unlikely that the team dedicated to tracking down and dismantling Iraq's war machine will ever be able to say they have completed their task.

For those that fought to free Kuwait the satisfaction of success lives on, however the achievement is regarded two years later. Simply, they were there. For the 40,000 British troops there are new battles—this time for their very existence. The Ministry of Defence's decision to use the end of the Cold War as the excuse to slim down the Army, in particular, has been hugely resented. Those who returned heroes from the Gulf were to find that mergers and amalgamations between regiments threatened not just centuries old traditions but livelihoods too. The Royal Scots and the Lifeguards (to name but two) who fought with distinction in the desert have found that it counts for nothing in these new, Treasury-driven days of retrenchment. A service medal finally distributed a year after the war is little compensation.

For the journalists, like myself privileged to be there, nastier conflicts were just around the corner. None died covering the Gulf conflict, from Kuwait's invasion to Iraq's expulsion. But in Yugoslavia, more anarchy than warfare, the toll was terrible. In Sarajevo alone, where I dodged more bullets in one day than I did in the entire desert war, more correspondents have been killed than in the

146

# POSTSCRIPT

entire 13 years of the Vietnam War. From royal correspondent to war correspondent has been an extraordinary experience. For me, prosaically it has continued, charging from war zone to palace party with flak jacket and tails ready by turn.

# GLOSSARY

*A10s.* US combat aircraft known as tankbusters or warthogs. Also F15s, fighter aircraft.

*AK 47.* Kalashnikov automatic rifle.

*Atrophine.* Anti-nerve gas solution.

*BAA.* Brigade Administrative Area.

*BFPO.* British Forces Post Office.

*BV.* Boiling vessel, for tea, coffee and boil in the bag food.

*Bereseford Flask.* Urinal device fitted to Warriors.

*Berms.* Border fortifications builts from the desert. Also revetments where Iraqis dug themselves in.

*Black Adder Lines.* Receiving point for newly arrived British troops. Named after TV comedy.

*Brewing up.* Exploding from inside out. What happens to a tank or APC when struck by armour piercing shells.

*Brews.* The stream of tea and coffee that sustained the troops.

*CARM.* Chemical agent repellant material, like reinforced plastic sheeting.

*CLAW* Close assault weapon. Rifle-fired grenade.

*CQMS.* Company quarter master sergeants.

*Challenger.* British tank.

*Compo.* Army rations.

*Compopen.* Syringe for infecting atrophine.

*DPs.* Desert pattern army fatigues.

*Desert rose.* Home made urinal.

*Dhahran.* Northern Saudi Arabian oil city and home to thousands of servicemen and journalists.

*Dib-dibbah.* The sand and gravel ground over which the war was found.

*FOO.* Forward observation officer in charge of artillery.

*FTU.* Forward Transmission Unit from where copy and film was sent to London.

*FTX.* Forward training exercise.

*FUP.* forming up position for attack.

*Facines.* Pipes used to fill obstacles like ditches.

*Gash pits.* Trenches dug in the desert to burn off rubbish.

*Giant viper.* Mine clearing explosive.

*Harbour party.* Advance guard.

*Humvey.* US military vehicle, successor to jeep.

*IRN.* Independent Radio News.

*JIB.* Joint Information Bureau. Set up by Britain and the US to brief correspondents.

*Law 80.* Shoulder-fired anti-tank missile (British).

*Lynx.* British Army helicopter. Also Puma.

*M1A1.* US tank. Also Abrams, US armoured personnel carrier.

*MLRS.* Multi launch rocket system.

*MOD.* Ministry of Defence.

*MRE.* Meals ready to eat, American staple diet.

*MRT.* Mobile Reporting Teams.

*MTLB.* Iraqi armoured personnel carrier. Also D20 and D30, artillery pieces and SA13, anti aircraft cannon.

*Magellan.* Electronic, self-correcting way-finder.

*Milan.* British wire-guided missile.

*NAAFI.* Canteen for servicemen. Literally Navy, Army, Air Force Institute.

*NAPS.* Nerve agent pre-treatment, or anti-nerve gas pills.

*NBC suits.* Nuclear, biological and chemical protection suits - required wearing for all Gulf soldiers.

*O Group.* Orders meeting.

*POW.* Prisoner of War. Also EPW, enemy prisoner of war.

*PX.* US post exchange. The American Naafi

*Patriot.* US missile interceptors.

*Ptarmigan.* Army's secure radio telephone line.

*R & R.* Recreation and recuperation. Vogue term since Vietnam war.

*REME.* Royal Electrical and Mechanical Engineers.

*REMFS.* Rear echelon mother fuckers. Also ACRS. Air conditioned remfs.

*RP.* Receiving point. Gaterhing place for a unit.

*RPG.* Rocket propelled grenade (Iraqi).

*Rarden gun.* 30 mm cannon fitted to Warrior.

*Republican Guard.* Saddam's elite force.

*Rolling replen.* Convoys that replenish food and ammunition for the front.

*Rufty-tufty.*The correspondents not attached to army units who roughed it alone.

*SA 80.* Literally small arms for the 80s. British Army issue automatic rifle.

*Safwan.* Iraqi border town where ceasefire was signed.

*Scrim net.* Army issue camouflage netting.

*Septics.* Rhyming slang for American troops. Septic tanks - Yanks.

*Shemagh.* Arab headress.

*Stags.* Staggered duties for day and night shift pattern.

*Step-up.* Shadow headquarters in case of attack.

*T55.* Iraq's principal front line tank. Soviet-built. Also T62, more updated.

*Tornado GR1 and F3.* Britain's main strike aircraft.

*Wadi al Batin.* Natural depression in the desert forming the border between Iraq, Kuwait and Saudi Arabia.

*Warrior.* Britain's armoured infantry carrier.

*Zero to three.* US Marines-speak for haircutting. Zero is short, three a scalping.